MANY WAYS TO LEARN

A Kid's Guide to LD

SECOND EDITION

MANY WAYS TO LEARN

A Kid's Guide to LD

SECOND EDITION

by Judith M. Stern, MA, and Uzi Ben-Ami, PhD

illustrated by Carl Pearce

MAGINATION PRESS • WASHINGTON, DC

American Psychological Association

Published by
MAGINATION PRESS
An Educational Publishing Foundation Book
American Psychological Association
750 First Street, NE
Washington, DC 20002

For more information about our books, including a complete catalog,
please write to us, call 1-800-374-2721, or visit our website at
www.apa.org/pubs/magination.

Book and cover design by Susan K. White
Printed by Worzalla, Stevens Point, Wisconsin

Library of Congress Cataloging-in-Publication Data
Stern, Judith M.
Many ways to learn : a kid's guide to LD / by Judith M. Stern
    and Uzi Ben-Ami ;
    illustrated by Carl Pearce. — 2nd ed.
    p. cm.
ISBN-13: 978-1-4338-0739-8 (hardcover : alk. paper)
ISBN-10: 1-4338-0739-4 (hardcover : alk. paper)
ISBN-13: 978-1-4338-0740-4 (pbk. : alk. paper)
ISBN-10: 1-4338-0740-8 (pbk. : alk. paper)
1. Learning disabilities—Juvenile literature. 2. Learning disabled
    children—Education—Juvenile literature. 3. Study skills—Juvenile
    literature. [1. Learning disabilities.] I. Ben-Ami, Uzi. II. Chesworth,
    Michael, ill. III. Title.
LC4704.S75 2010
371.9—dc22   2010023125

First printing September 2010

10 9 8 7 6 5 4 3 2 1

In loving memory of
Richard Holcombe
and
for Shoshana Ben-Ami,
a dedicated,
beloved teacher.

Introduction to Parents

This second edition of *Many Ways to Learn* is written for children like yours—kids with learning disabilities (LD). Reading it will arm them with the tools they need to help themselves in school, at home, and with other kids. The book has been greatly expanded from the first edition to provide a clear and positive understanding of living with LD. It offers lots of practical tips and strategies to take on everyday obstacles that are specific to each kind of LD. It will also help kids

- explore and understand their strengths and weaknesses;
- examine their own learning and work styles to increase their confidence and optimism in school;
- develop strategies that will help them make friends and improve their self-esteem—in and out of the classroom; and
- build a support team—you and others—who will work with them to overcome the challenges they face.

This book is written for kids, but parents, teachers, and counselors may use it to find child-friendly ways to explain learning disabilities and discover new ways to support children with LD. One of the best things you can do is to remind your children of their strengths—they have plenty—and to guide them through their challenges. No matter how old your child is—or what kind of LD he or she has—you will be a significant member of the climbing team.

We hope you enjoy the part of the climb you take together.

Contents

The Climb Starts Here

Dealing with a learning disability (or LD) can feel like climbing a mountain. The path might seem rocky and difficult. You may sometimes feel lost or confused. But you can also have a lot of fun climbing. You can enjoy the beautiful scenery around you, and you can look down and see how far up you have come. When you have finished your climb, you will feel proud of how strong and capable you really are!

Imagine this: When you begin to climb a mountain, you look up and see how far you have to go. That may seem overwhelming! The equipment you carry feels heavy and uncomfortable. But your desire to reach the top of the mountain will help you find the strength to make it all the way. Your good attitude and effort will power your legs, arms, and mind. And you'll figure out many ways to make your climb easier and fun. After a while, you know that you will make it!

You also know that you never have to climb alone. You're climbing with a team of experienced guides who will help you. When you have LD, parents, teachers, counselors, and tutors are like your climbing support team. Your good friends encourage you when the path becomes rough. They celebrate your accomplishments with you. Having company and support is the best way to climb!

There are many ways to climb a mountain, just as there are many ways to learn and enjoy school. This book is your guide to getting started. Think of it as your climbing guide.

You're probably reading this book because you've been told that you have LD. When you have LD, one of the best things you can do for yourself is to find out what it means. Then you can take steps to help yourself work successfully with your LD.

Before you start reading, here are some ways you might want to use the book:

- You don't have to read it from cover to cover. You can jump around or go straight to the information you want and need. Some parts of the book may not apply to you. You may choose to skip over them and come back at another time.
- Even though something might not seem like it applies to you, consider checking it out. You might learn something new that could help you.
- If something in the book isn't clear, ask someone else what it means. Your parents, teachers, tutor, and counselors can help with this.
- If you find information that seems especially important to you, make a note of it with a highlighter or a sticky flag so you can continue to think about it later.
- You may want to share this book with your parents, teachers, counselor, or friends so they can better understand you and find out how they can best support you.

We've worked with many children who have LD. We hope to share with you ideas that have worked well for them. We believe that one of the most important parts of understanding your LD is to look at all that you can do, and continue to strengthen those skills.

This book will help you to find your strengths and develop them. It will also show you many good ways to improve your ability to learn. Using information from this book and the support of your family, friends, and other important people in your life, you'll be on your way to working with your LD and feeling great about yourself.

We wish you a good climb as you find your way up the mountain!

PART 1

FACING THE MOUNTAIN: FINDING OUT ABOUT LD

C H A P T E R 1
What Is LD?

A simple way to describe learning disabilities (LD) is to say that you have difficulties learning one or more school subjects, though you can learn other subjects more easily. Another way to describe LD is if you have received extra help at school in your difficult subjects, and you still have trouble learning them. Some people look at LD another way. For them, LD means learning differences—how each individual learns best in different ways. Some kids understand a book best when it is read out loud to them. Other kids need to be in a quiet room reading to themselves.

Millions of people around the country and all over the world have LD. In the United States alone, more than 4,500,000 children have some form of LD. Both girls and boys have LD, and adults have them, too. So as you can see, if you have LD, it's not just you! Plenty of other kids in your school, on your sports teams, and in your neighborhood may also have LD.

What Kinds of LD Are There?

A difficulty in a school subject may be connected to one or more of these problems:
• Trouble understanding things people say
• Trouble speaking (oral language LD)
• Difficulty reading
• Difficulty writing
• Difficulty spelling
• Trouble listening

- Difficulty doing math
- Trouble with non-verbal skills

In Part 3 of the book, we'll look at each learning problem in more detail. First, let's take a quick peek at each of them so you get an idea.

Reading LD

Kids with reading LD may have a hard time with some of these:

- Reading letters with their correct sounds
- Sounding out words
- Easily recognizing sight words, such as *said* or *their*
- Keeping their place on the words on a page while reading
- Understanding what they have read

Math LD

Kids with math LD may have difficulty with some of these:

- Learning and remembering math facts
- Doing math calculations quickly and without mistakes
- Solving word problems
- Learning new ideas in math, such as counting money or understanding fractions

Written Language LD

Kids with written language LD may have a hard time with some of these:

- Writing their ideas in sentences or paragraphs
- Organizing ideas so that their sentences make sense
- Spelling correctly
- Writing as fast as other kids in their class

Oral Language LD

Kids with oral language LD may have a hard time with some or all of these:

- Saying out loud what they are thinking
- Organizing words and ideas so that others understand what they mean
- Thinking of the right words to use
- Using new vocabulary words
- Putting their words in the right order when speaking

Non-Verbal LD

People think some thoughts without using words. This is called "non-verbal thinking." People with non-verbal LD (NLD) have a hard time figuring out things that have to do with non-verbal thinking.

For example, let's say you are on a sports team. Many of the moves you decide to make may be done without thinking in words. You picture certain things in your mind and figure out which is the best move to help your team.

Here's another example. Did you ever watch someone fix a car? That person may use non-verbal skills to figure out what is wrong with the car and what needs to be changed without using any words.

Climbing BREAK

The Eagle and the Mountain Lion

Here's another way to think about learning differences. Think about the eagle and the mountain lion. The eagle's brain is better at understanding what it sees from far away, like where it can look for its next meal. The mountain lion's brain is better at understanding the tiniest sounds it hears from the bushes and the scents of other animals. Each of these animals has its own strengths and weaknesses. The eagle doesn't have as strong a sense of smell as the lion. The mountain lion cannot see as well from the distance as the eagle. Each of them can survive in the mountains very well. Just like the eagle or the mountain lion, people have weaknesses and strengths. You can be sure that for each of your learning weaknesses, you have an important learning strength. One way or another, you will find your best way to learn!

Kids with non-verbal LD may have a hard time with some or all of the following:

- Organization skills
- Balance and coordination
- Working quickly
- Understanding situations that involve other people
- Finding their way around a place without getting lost

Climbing BREAK

Lots of famous and successful people have had LD. Here are some:

- Albert Einstein, a scientific genius, needed more time to learn his math facts than other students in his class.
- Sir Winston Churchill, Prime Minister of Britain during World War II, had a difficult time learning in school.
- Tommy Hilfiger, the fashion designer, has LD.
- Bruce Jenner, an Olympic decathlon champion and one of the world's greatest athletes, had a reading LD as a child.
- Agatha Christie, the best-selling writer of books of all time, according to the *Guinness Book of World Records*, was a horrible speller and had such terrible handwriting that she didn't begin to write her books until she could type.

We know plenty of kids with LD who have grown up and done very, very well! Don't let learning problems stop you. With hard work, you can accomplish so much!

What LD Kids Are Not

Let's admit it. If you have LD, you do have trouble learning some school subjects and may have other difficulties outside of school. But what we know for certain is that:

• You are not lazy.
• You are not stupid.
• You are not going to fail.
• You need extra help, but that's okay.

What Do I Need to Know About My Brain?

The brain is where all learning and thinking take place. The brain is made up of billions of cells called neurons. Messages with thoughts and commands travel over tiny spaces between neurons called synapses and pass from one neuron to another. These messages control everything you do!

To solve a new math problem in school, many different parts of your brain need to work together. This brain activity lets you

• Look at the board;
• Listen to the teacher;
• Understand what the teacher says;
• Write down the steps the teacher is showing; and
• Remember it all!

Your brain controls all of these steps. Depending on what you learn, different areas of the brain will be working. If you're learning math, different areas of the brain will be at work than when you're learning how to sound out new words in reading.

Not everyone's brain works the same way. This is normal and explains why one child is good at some things and not at others. Do you know someone who is a great chess player? A wonderful horseback rider? A talented artist? Each of them is probably less good in doing other things. If you have LD, your brain is good at learning some things, even though your brain has a hard time learning other subjects.

Compensation

Good news! Your brain is smart enough to help when you have trouble learning anything. So, if you have a hard time learning something, another part of your brain can help a specific part to learn something new. This is called compensation.

For example, using your hands together with your eyes may help you figure out a math problem more easily. You still learn to solve the math problem, just in a different way. You do what you need to do in another way that works better for you.

How Did I Get LD?

LD is something you're born with. It often runs in families. A child with LD may have one or more relatives who also have LD. If other members of your family have LD, they might help you understand and work with your LD. It is also possible that no one else in your family has LD, even if you do.

There are different kinds of LD, and we talked about them in this chapter. You will learn more about them later in the book. Millions of people in the United States have LD and people all around the world also have them. In the next chapter, we'll talk about the problems that sometimes go along with LD.

CHAPTER 2
What Problems Can Be Part of LD?

N o matter what kind of LD you have, some problems make it more difficult to learn. In this chapter, we will talk about some of these problems. As you read, try to see which ones apply to you. Here are problems that often go with some LD:

- Language Problems
- Visual-Processing Problems
- Motor Problems
- Visual-Motor Problems
- Cognitive Problems

We'll talk about each of these problems in this chapter and the next one.

Language Problems

Language problems are problems with speaking or understanding what you read or hear. Language problems can show up in your speech, writing, and reading. Sometimes it may be hard to use language when you are putting your ideas into writing or talking to someone else. It may be hard to understand what things mean when you listen to others or read. For example,

- You have difficulty understanding what you hear or what you read.
- When people tell you something, you may need to have it repeated or explained in a different way.

- You may need extra time to form your answer when someone asks you a question.
- When you speak or write, you have trouble putting your ideas into words so people know what you are thinking.
- Your ideas come out in a disorganized way.

It can be frustrating when you can't say what you really mean. This may happen when you are trying to explain something to your friends or parents or when you are trying to write an assignment. Sometimes kids with this problem don't tell as much as they really know when they write because writing just feels too hard for them.

Visual-Processing Problems

Visual processing has to do with what you see. The brain takes information that your eyes see and tries to figure out what it means. If you have difficulty with visual-processing, you may recognize one or more of these problems from your own life:

- You have trouble seeing differences between shapes, letters, words, or numbers.
- You see the letters in a word in the wrong order, such as reading *there* as *three*.
- You confuse words that look alike, such as *cool* and *coal* or *list* and *last*.
- You skip words when you read.
- You become confused (and maybe tired) when you look at a page that has a lot of writing.

If visual-processing skills are hard for you, people may think you are being careless even when you really are trying hard to do the right thing. You may have to slow down when you work and check everything carefully to find mistakes.

Motor Problems

"Motor skills" is another name for how we use our muscles. If someone has a problem using different kinds of muscles, we say that they have motor problems. We use our muscles for two main kinds of activity:

• Gross motor skills, which use our muscles to do big movements (such as running or swimming)

• Fine motor skills, which use our hand and finger muscles (such as tying shoes or working with clay)

If you have problems with gross or fine motor skills, you might have some of the following problems.

• Trouble cutting with scissors
• Tripping a lot when you run or walk
• Having a hard time sewing or using tweezers or a screwdriver
• Difficulty catching or hitting a ball with a bat or racquet
• Taking a long time to learn to ride a bike

Visual-Motor Problems

Most motor skills require you to use your eyes together with your muscles. These are called "visual-motor skills." Some kids with LD may have trouble with gross motor or fine motor skills because their eyes don't work well together with their muscle movements. Here are some examples where the eyes and hands must work together as a team:

• Writing letters and numbers clearly
• Staying on the line when you write
• Copying words or numbers from the board or from a book
• Drawing
• Pouring liquid into a cup

It may take longer to develop some of the motor skills, but with extra help you can get better. Playing sports is a fun way to practice gross motor skills. So are dancing and swimming lessons.

Putting together models, doing crafts, knitting, and painting are great ways to practice fine motor skills and have fun. Remember the mountain climber who has plenty of practice before making any big climb!

Many kids with LD have good motor skills, while others may have problems with gross or fine motor skills. If you are lucky enough to be strong in these areas, it may help you in your learning. (We know kids who like to study while using an exercise bicycle!)

Cognitive Problems

Cognitive skills are the brain skills that we use to learn and know things. In order to learn and know, we need to be able to:

- Reason (figure out and solve problems)
- Remember and use information
- Get organized
- Pay attention
- Work at a reasonable speed

Some kids with LD have problems with cognitive skills such as:

- Difficulties with reasoning. If it's hard for you to solve different kinds of problems, you may have difficulties with reasoning. It may be hard to do math problems or predict the end of a story.

Climbing BREAK

Do you know any kids like these?

- Jeffie found a 4-week-old tuna sandwich in the bottom of his backpack. He said, "Oh, that's where it went!"

- Daisy had 3 weeks to work on her book report. She started it the night before. Guess what her mom said to her that night?

- Oscar spent 2 hours doing his homework. When he got to school the next day, he realized that all of his work was still on the kitchen table. Oh, Oscar!

- When something does not work the first time, it may be hard for you to figure out another way to make it work.
- Slow processing speed. This means you have problems working quickly. You may be able to learn and work well, but only if you have extra time.

Another problem with cognitive skills has to do with memory.

Memory Problems

If you have memory problems, you may:
- Have difficulties remembering what you learned;
- Take a long time remembering the correct spelling of words, math facts, or social studies information; or
- Start saying something, and then forget what you were talking about.

If you have memory problems, you may have to work extra hard. You may need to write things down or keep a list so you don't forget important things. Plenty of people have trouble with memory and think of good ways to help themselves. We know a boy who leaves himself notes in his lunchbox so he doesn't forget what he needs to bring home that afternoon.

Executive Function Difficulties

Executive functions are the jobs that your brain does to help you with organization, sense of time, and planning skills. Executive function difficulties may make it hard for you to:
- Get started on work
- Stay on task
- Finish work
- Do your work neatly

- Remember to do your work or chores
- Manage big projects and assignments

Executive function difficulties can affect your life inside and outside of school. Losing things, whether it's your homework or a favorite jacket, can feel pretty bad. Luckily, there are lots of ways to manage these problems. You'll learn ways to get better organized later in this book.

Attention Problems

Kids with attention-deficit/hyperactivity disorder (ADHD) have many problems with paying attention and staying focused. They get distracted easily and often cannot stay on one activity long enough to finish it. For example, kids with ADHD may have trouble reading a chapter or solving several math problems in a row without switching to another activity that they shouldn't be doing. Some kids (but not all) may have trouble with hyperactivity which means they move around a lot. Sometimes ADHD causes hard times with:

- Sitting still
- Thinking before acting
  - Getting good grades (because it is hard to start or finish schoolwork)
       Kids with ADHD often improve when they receive extra home and school help and learn ways to focus better. Medication for ADHD can also help. Not all kids with ADHD have LD, but many do. The people who check to see if you have LD may also check to see if you have attention problems.

In the next chapter, you will learn how kids find out if they have LD.

CHAPTER 3
How Do I Know
If I Have LD?

So how do you find out if you actually have LD? In this chapter we'll talk about the people who work together to figure out if you have LD and how they do it. We'll also discuss what your parents and teachers do once they figure out if you have LD. Here are the steps to find out if you have LD:

- You, your parents, or your teachers feel that something about learning is hard for you.
- People at your school try extra hard to help you learn more easily.
- If extra help doesn't make enough of a difference, you get tested.
- Your parents and teachers then meet together to talk about the results of the special testing.
- A plan is written for you. Hopefully, someone explains that plan to you, because you are part of your learning team.

Here are more details about each step.

Learning Is Hard for You

What does it mean when people notice that learning is hard for you? Some of these examples may help explain:

- If you are in sixth grade, but you can do only third grade math, you and your teachers decide that math is a hard subject for you.
- Whenever you do a homework writing assignment, your parents see

that you get really frustrated.

- You are smart, but very disorganized at school and home, so your grades are poor.

Once your parents, teachers, or counselor notice your difficulty, they will have a discussion with people at school about what is hard for you. They may suggest that the school try some new ways to teach you. Schools call this Response to Intervention, which means they want to see if your learning improves once you have the extra help.

If the extra help was not enough, your parents or school may check to see if you have LD. There are special kinds of tests that check how you learn and why you have difficulties learning.

Climbing BREAK

Learning Styles

Everyone has a different way of learning. These are called learning styles. There are many ways to learn. Here are some examples:

- Some kids learn best when using their eyes. This is visual learning.
- Some kids learn best when using their ears. This is auditory learning.
- Some kids learn best by doing things using their hands and other parts of the body. This is kinesthetic learning.
- Most kids learn best by using some or all of these learning styles.

Guess what is a dog's best learning style? Sniffing!

You Take Some Tests

When kids are tested for LD, they take more than one special test, because there is no single test for LD. Most of the tests check how you learn and how well you are doing in school so far. We'll talk more about these tests now.

Learning and Achievement Tests

LD tests are given by people who know a great deal about learning. They check to see what types of learning are hard for you, and what you are able to do well. Because these people are used to working with kids, they are kind and make kids feel comfortable taking tests.

When some people hear the word "tests", they worry because they think about grades. But LD testing is not about grades. It's about figuring out your strengths and weaknesses and what kind of help you need. Many kids find LD tests fun to take. Best of all, you don't need to study for them at all!

Most of the time, the people doing the tests will look at your skills in:

• Reading
• Math
• Writing
• Language
• Listening
• Copying
• Attention
• Work speed

You may also be asked questions to find out how you feel about school and learning. Because parents and teachers want you to feel good about yourself, this is a good way to find out what you have been thinking.

Once you've finished all the tests, the school may still want to know how well and how quickly you solve problems and remember information. In that case, you will also take an intelligence test. If you are given an intelligence test, here is what you should know about it.

Intelligence Tests

Intelligence tests are used to estimate how well and how quickly you learn new things, how well you remember things, how well you solve problems, and how quickly you do them. All of these are part of what we call **intelligence**.

Intelligence tests do not tell how smart you are in all areas of your life. They do not tell how well you can do outside of school or how well you will succeed in life. They do not tell how hard you can work or how well you listen or how organized you are in school. They tell nothing about how good a friend you are, or how you do in sports or art. All of these qualities can be just as important as doing well in school subjects and they are not part of intelligence testing. Intelligence tests measure only a small part of how capable you are.

What Happens After the Testing Is Finished?

When you finish the testing, all the results and other information are put together to see if you have LD. The people who tested you are then ready to share this information with your parents and teachers, who decide together what will make learning easier for you. They do this at a special school meeting.

School Meetings

In public schools, your parents, teachers, guidance counselor, principal, and school psychologist meet together to decide if you need special help. If they agree that you have LD, they make a plan for how to best teach you. This is called an **IEP**, which stands for an **Individualized Educational Plan**. Each child with LD has his or her own personal IEP that tells the teacher what kind of help will make it easier for you to learn, and what you will need in order to improve reading, math, writing, or language.

Knowledge is power, like the strength you need to pull yourself up on a mountain climb. Knowing that you have LD will allow you to do something about it! In the next chapter, we'll talk about people who can help you do that—they are your climbing team.

CHAPTER 4
Who's on My Climbing Team?

When you climb a mountain, it is easier when you do it with a climbing team. People help each other, solve problems together, and encourage each other to keep climbing. Kids with LD have their own climbing teams. These are people who help when things get tough and work with you to make learning easier. For many kids, parents, teachers, and counselors make up their team. Because no two kids are alike, climbing teams are not always alike either. Let's look at different team members and how they help kids.

Parents

Parents know their kids very well and care about them. They understand your LD and want to do things that will help you do well in and out of school. Many parents are willing to help their kids study for tests, and explain homework. At school meetings, they tell teachers about some of the things you need. Your parents listen to you and figure out ways to help. You can talk to your parents about:

- How to make homework easier for you;
- How to set up your room and workspace in a way that works well;
- How brothers, sisters, and friends help or interfere with your life;
- What you like and don't like about school; and
- After-school activities you want to do.

Climbing KIT

Talk to Your Parents

Here are some tips to use when you talk to your parents about your LD:

- Ask your parents for the best time for them to listen to you.
- Make a list of what you want to talk about.
- Take a deep breath before you start talking.
- Explain what you need and suggest solutions, instead of complaining.

Family Members

Along with your parents or guardians, you probably have family members who are really close to you. They might include:

- Grandparents
- Aunts and uncles
- Brothers and sisters
- Stepfamily
- Cousins

Each family member can help you in different ways. We know a boy who has an aunt who is an actress. Sometimes they read books together, because the aunt makes funny accents, which makes books come alive. Which family members are on your climbing team?

Teachers

Teachers work with you in school. The more they work with you, the better they know what you need to be a successful learner. Many teachers are willing to try new ways to make learning easier for you. Here are some things they may do:

- Meet with you after class to go over schoolwork.
- Make directions easier to understand.
- Let you try some different ways to work.
- Give you extra help to prepare for a test.
- Find the best place for you to sit in class.

When you make progress in school, teachers cheer along with you!

Learning Specialists

Learning specialists are teachers who work with students who need extra help with a subject. In some schools, these teachers are called resource teachers. They find out what works best for each student, instead of trying to teach everyone the same way. They also give your teachers ideas to try out with you.

Sometimes you work with a learning specialist or a resource teacher in their office, which may be called a resource room. In many schools, the learning specialist comes right into the classroom to help you and some of your classmates during class. You'll work with a learning specialist on:

• Classwork and homework that is hard for you;

• Improving your skills in reading, math, or writing;

• Managing big projects or assignments;

• Studying for tests; and

• Organizing homework.

Classes or Schools for Kids With LD

If you are in a class just for kids with LD or go to a special school for kids with LD, you may have more teacher specialists and smaller classes there. In these places, adults work with one another to make sure that you get plenty of help. That creates a very strong climbing team.

Tutors or Educational Therapists

If you work with a tutor, you know that he or she is good at explaining classwork or homework that may be difficult or

Kids' Climbing Teams

Your climbing team is important to you, both inside and outside of school. Here is what some kids say about their team members:

○ I meet twice a week with a math tutor.

○ I work with a speech-language pathologist to learn how to organize my ideas before I write them down.

○ My teacher spends a few minutes with me before I go home for the day to help me organize my homework.

○ My older brother tests me on my spelling words every Thursday and teaches me good tricks for remembering hard words.

What does your climbing team look like?

confusing for you. In some parts of the country, special tutors are called educational therapists. They all help you improve skills such as reading and math, and help you to prepare for tests and learn new ways to study.

Guidance Counselors

If your school has a guidance counselor, you know that this is a person who helps with personal or school problems. Guidance counselors try to help kids feel comfortable in school. They listen when you tell them about learning problems and what happens to you in school. You can also talk to them about other things, including:

• What helps you do well in school

• Problems with other kids

• How you feel about your teacher

• Problems if you are being teased or bullied

Guidance counselors work with your parents and teachers to make sure you feel good about school. Counselors are interested in how school is going, so make sure to let them know!

Therapists

Sometimes it helps to meet with a counselor or therapist outside of school. You can think of them as "feelings doctors." They give you a chance to discuss your feelings. They encourage you to talk about things that bother you (a bad grade? a fight with your sister? a bully?). A therapist or counselor is on your side and will try to help you, whatever the problem might be.

You may see a therapist by yourself, together with your family, or in a group with other kids. If you are feeling unhappy, a therapist may help you feel better about your life and teach you new ways to take care of yourself.

Coaches

Coaches work with one person at a time to help improve time management, organization, and other skills. A coach might help you keep up with a big assignment by checking in with you each day.

A coach can also help you:

• Organize your homework, bedroom, or book bag.

• Figure out a good after-school work schedule.

• Develop a plan for finishing big projects on time.

• Learn new ways to get ready for tests.

A coach is there to make your school life easier. How cool is that?

Speech-Language Pathologists

If you have problems pronouncing words or using language skills, you may work with a speech-language pathologist. These are specialists who know how to help kids and adults:

• Pronounce words more clearly.

• Organize ideas in sentences.

• Learn how to explain to other people what you need.

• Understand what people say.

Occupational Therapists

Kids who have trouble with some of their motor skills, like writing or running, may work with an occupational therapist to improve those skills. An occupational therapist helps with activities that involve fingers, arms, or whole body, so that you feel more comfortable with movement, balance, handwriting, and other physical activities. You have a good time while you get stronger. This is one place where you won't get into any trouble for moving around.

Now that you know more about LD and who can help, the next question is what can be done to make learning easier? The next part of the book is full of ideas for you.

PART 2

STARTING THE CLIMB: LIFE AT SCHOOL

CHAPTER 5
Getting a Leg up in School

Most kids spend at least 6 hours a day in school. That's a lot of time in one place! School should be a place where you feel comfortable and accepted. Climbing team members will help make your school days go well, so let them know what you need. **You** are the main mountain climber, so your ideas and hard work matter most. In this chapter, we'll explain how you can:

• Understand your strengths and weaknesses.
• Ask for school accommodations.
• Work with your climbing team.
• Talk to an adult at school.
• Learn in special classes.

Understand Your Strengths and Weaknesses

It really helps to understand your own learning strengths and weaknesses. Your strengths are things you're good at, and weaknesses are things you haven't become good at yet. Once you know what these are, you can use the information to improve your learning.

• If you learn best by listening, ask your teacher to let you audio-record test review lessons in class, so that you can use them for studying.
• If you are a good artist, drawing what you are reading about may help you remember facts or ideas.

When you know your weaknesses, you can work around them.

- If it is hard for you to memorize, ask your teacher to give you a test review sheet early, so you can get extra practice.
- If you make many mistakes in math, make sure to check over your work before handing it in. Some teachers will allow you to use a calculator to check your work.

Make a List

It is useful to make a list of your strengths and weaknesses. Try this:

- On a piece of paper, or on the computer, list your learning strengths and other things you are good at.
- Include school subjects you do well in and how you learn best.
- In the weakness section, list school subjects you find the hardest and what makes each subject hard for you.
- When you finish the list, ask everyone on your climbing team for more ideas to add to your list.

Now you will have a good picture of yourself as a learner. Show it to the people who work with you so they can help you use the list. If you'd like to see an example, look at Mala's list on the next page.

Ask About School Accommodations

When you and your teachers understand your LD, you will all be able to make some changes to help you in school. A change to help a student learn more easily is called an **accommodation**. Accommodations are written into your IEP. Many students with LD spend most of the school day in a regular classroom, where many of the other kids do not have LD. Students with LD do better in regular classes when they get the accommodations they need.

Climbing KIT

Mala's Learning Strengths and Weaknesses

STRENGTHS

I'm good at working with other kids.
I'm good at basketball.
I'm good at Math and PE.

Ways that I learn best:

Walking around while I study
Reading out loud so I can hear myself
Working in a group with other kids

The best ways for me to show that I have learned something:

Acting it out
Drawing it

WEAKNESSES

I don't pay attention really well.
I get frustrated when homework is hard.
I need the most help in reading. It's really hard for me!

Things that are hard for me to do in school:

Reading out loud in front of people
Listening to the teacher when she talks too much

I need more time to finish:

Science tests
Chapter books
Writing essays

Teachers know that children have many different ways of learning. They know that small accommodations can make a big difference. For example, a teacher may have you use a different spelling book or let you use the computer to write your social studies essay.

In-Class Accommodations

Here are some accommodations that we have seen on kids' IEPs:

- Writing answers next to the questions instead of on an answer sheet;
- Having less homework in a difficult subject;
- Dictating quiz or test answers to your teacher;
- Using a calculator to check math work;
- Sitting near the teacher or where there is less distraction; and
- Getting homework a few days early so you have extra days to do it.

Testing Accommodations

If you work slowly, you may need more time to finish tests in school. Allowing more time to finish tests, called **extended time testing**, is an accommodation the school may give if they think you need it.

Work With Your Climbing Team

Help is all around you! Here are some ways you can work with your climbing team:

- Tell your teacher if you have been spending too much time on homework. She might be willing to cut down the amount you have to do.

- Tell your parents what kind of supplies you need in order to keep your school papers better organized.
- Tell your soccer coach what will make you feel more in control during the game. You can work out a special signal to use when you need another set of directions.
- Let your friends know what works for you when you get together, like taking turns deciding what you will play.

If you know what works for you, make sure to let everyone know.

Talk to an Adult at School

So, your day started with your spelling homework going to another school in your older sister's backpack by mistake, but your teacher does not believe it. Then your little brother comes to your class to remind you (in his loud voice) to hand in your field trip permission slip, because your mother was afraid you would forget it. Your friend sat on your peanut butter and jelly sandwich on the bus. Now you have no lunch and he has a stain on his pants.

Instead of punching your backpack, it might feel good to talk to someone who gives extra support when you really need it. Life at school may feel easier if you find at least one adult who helps when you need advice on a school problem or help getting through a bad day. No one can help every time something goes wrong, but it's good to know who to

go to when you really need it. Talking out a problem may help you get on track and back to class faster. Is there someone in your school you can talk to? Figure out with that person the best thing to do when you feel you need to talk.

Learning in Special Classes

You may receive extra help for your LD at school by working with a resource teacher. They usually work with students alone or in small groups, from one-half hour a week to several hours a day.

You may spend most of your school day in a class with a special teacher who works only with students who have LD. Most of your school subjects are studied in this classroom, although you may also be partly mainstreamed. This means that you leave your classroom and go into other regular classrooms for some of your subjects, such as math or PE.

In the next chapter, we'll talk about everyone's favorite topic—homework (not!). We'll share some ideas for getting homework done. So read on.

CHAPTER 6

Homework and Tests

A re you one of those kids who would rather play baseball than do homework? Hang out with friends instead of studying for next week's test? Can you believe there are actually ways to do both? In this chapter, we'll review some ideas for managing homework and tests.

Homework Strategies

Yes, there is life after homework, but first you must get that homework done. Try some of these suggestions so that the "H word" does not make you scream. We'll talk about

- Remembering assignments
- Getting organized
- Getting homework done
- Choosing a homework buddy
- Rewarding yourself

Remembering Assignments

Can't remember what your social studies homework is? Thought that the book report wasn't due until Friday, but it was really due 2 days before (OOPS!)? Here are some ways you can remember your assignments and get them done in time:

- Use a homework planner or assignment book. Write down assignments each day and look them over when you get home.
- Before leaving school, look over your planner to bring the right things home.

- Before packing up at night, check your assignment book again to make sure everything is finished.
- If your school has a homework hotline or teacher web pages, use them.
- If there are books or things, like calculators, that you always need to bring home, make yourself a colorful list of those items and hang the list in your locker or put it on your notebook cover.
- Check in with your homework buddy. (We'll talk about that soon.)

How can you organize your time?

Getting Organized

Does it feel like homework spreads out and swallows your free time? Here are some tips to help you stay organized, manage time, and start mornings in a happier way!

- When you get home from school, make a schedule for that night. Include chores and after-school activities in the schedule. Now you know how much free time you can plug in for that day.
- After a long day at at school, get some exercise before starting homework. It helps you feel good and focus better.
- Figure out the best time to do your homework. Some kids like to come home and get started right away while still in a "school mood." Other kids like to take free time right after school and then begin homework.

We work with lots of kids, so we know how most kids feel about homework. But the truth is that once you work hard and finish it, you can really, really enjoy yourself. So have a good attitude and watch what happens. Let's look at some other homework suggestions.

Getting Homework Done

Doing homework can be easier if you try some of these things.

- If you have trouble with homework directions, work with a climbing team member (by phone or in person) to make sure you know what to do before starting.
- Do homework in a place that has the fewest distractions. Get away from the TV, the phone, and your crying baby brother.
- If you go to an after-school program, finish some assignments there.
- If you have study hall during school, start homework there. When you get home, you will have less to do.
- Some kids like to do easy homework first. Others like to get the hardest assignments finished first. Which works for you?
- Break a difficult assignment into several parts. After you complete each part, take a short break before continuing.
- If you're spending too much time on homework each night, talk to your teacher. Some teachers will reduce assignments if they know that a student's LD makes it harder to do an assignment. Some teachers may give you extra time to finish.

Climbing KIT

Sample Project Schedule

Anneke has a big science project. She decided to do a small part each day. Here is her plan:

Mon.: Choose topic.

Tues.: Read chapter 4 in science textbook.

Wed.: Research topic online and in library.

Thur.: Take research notes.

Sat.: Write outline for essay.

Sun.: Write essay.

Mon.: Hand in rough draft.

Tues.: Day off while teacher checks the rough draft!

Wed.: Make corrections on draft and finish essay.

Thur.: Hand in final essay.

Choosing a Homework Buddy

A homework buddy is someone in your class who can help you if you're not sure you wrote down all the assignments or have a homework question. Your buddy can explain confusing directions and help you study for tests. Think about who would be a good homework buddy:

• Pick someone who is organized.

• Find someone who you get along with.

• If you go to different classes during the day, find a homework buddy for each class.

If you can't find a homework buddy, ask your teacher for suggestions.

Rewarding Yourself

Sometimes a reward at the end of a big job helps us feel better about finishing. Did you ever watch how your favorite sports team celebrates after they win a big game?

• Promise yourself small rewards for completing each assignment. ("When I finish math, I will move around and get a snack.")

• Plan bigger rewards for completing homework on time. ("When all my homework is done, I'll shoot hoops with Dad.")

• Work with your parents to set up some homework rewards.

Test Strategies

Doing well on tests takes work, no matter how smart you are. That means studying hard and learning how to take different kinds of tests. Let's talk about:

• Getting organized for tests

• Studying for tests

• Taking tests

• Managing essay tests

Getting Organized for Tests

Do you stay up late the night before tests? Maybe it's because you often forget to study in advance. If you organize your time well, you are better prepared and less stressed when studying. Here's what you can do:

- Start studying for tests many days before they will be given so you feel confident and prepared the day of the test.
- Figure out what you need to concentrate. You might do better sitting at a desk or lying on the floor when you study.
- Pay attention to the time of day when you concentrate best. If you do better in the morning, try studying on weekends when your mornings belong to you.

Studying for Tests

There are so many ways to study for tests. Some are listed here.
Ask your teachers and parents for other ideas.

- Make study cards. Put a vocabulary word, math or social studies fact on the front. On the back, put the definition or answer. Test yourself from either side of the card later.
- When you take notes in class, write only on the first half of the page. Use the second half of each page to write summary notes to prepare for a test. Read the summary notes at the end of the day.
- Speak information into an audio recorder and listen to it over and over.
- Instead of memorizing entire sentences, select key words that you need to learn. For example: rice – crop – China from "Rice is the most important crop in China."

- Make a word or words out of the first letters of the items you are trying to memorize. This is called a **mnemonic**. Mnemonics are tricks that you can use to memorize things. To remember the four oceans (Indian, Arctic, Atlantic, Pacific), you can remember "**I A**m **A P**erson."
- Try forming a picture in your mind of what you are studying so you can remember the image when you need it. Practice with this: Mercury is the planet closest to the Sun.

Climbing
BREAK

Funny Mnemonics

To remember the continents:

(**A**sia, **N**orth America, **S**outh America, **A**frica, **E**urope, **A**ustralia, and **A**ntarctica) make up and memorize a funny sentence with each word starting with the beginning letter of one of the continents:

Here's one: "**A**ardvarks **n**ever **s**wim **af**ter **e**ating **a**mazing **a**nts."

So you've studied hard and feel confident. The next step is to know how to handle tests once they are on your desk.

Taking Tests

There are some common sense rules for taking tests carefully.

- Before starting any test section, read directions over twice.

- Don't spend too much time on any one question or section. If you have trouble with a question, make a mark next to it and come back to it later.
- Once you know how much time you have for a test, figure out how much time to spend on each part. Then you won't run out of time at the end.
- If you forget something you studied, use a blank piece of paper (with your teacher's permission) to write down everything that comes into your mind about the topic. If you relax, the ideas may come back to you.
- If long tests are hard for you, plan ahead with your teacher to take the test one page at a time, at different parts of the day, or even on different days.
- On multiple choice questions, try getting rid of answers you know are wrong so there are only a few choices left. (This is called the "process of elimination".) Here's one:

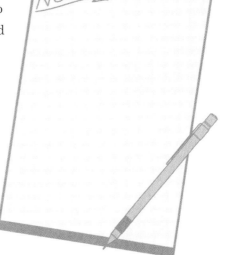

      The dolphin was _____.
             a) kneeling
             b) swimming
             c) shopping

Managing Essay Tests

Here are some things to know about essay tests.

- Make an outline or web before you write your answers. Plan which information you want to include. Write your outline in pencil, so you can erase and change.
- If you can use the computer, keyboard your essay.
- Check back to make sure you included all the information you wanted to use.
- Use a main idea and supporting details in each paragraph.
- In some classes, kids are allowed to give answers by telling them to the teacher at another time, or recording answers on an audio recorder.

Before handing in your essay, look for for mistakes.

- did you use capital letters Where they are Supposed to be?
- Does every sentence? have punctuation at the end

Maybe you like PE and Art better than homework and tests. But they are all part of school. With practice and hard work, you can learn to manage homework and tests. In the next chapter we'll talk about how to get organized and feel more in control.

CHAPTER 7

Organizing and Planning

D o you know where you left your favorite baseball glove? Do you remember when your science project is due? What time does your soccer tournament start on Saturday? Wow, you have a lot of things to keep track of! If you have a hard time keeping track of your stuff and your schedule, you're not alone. Many people have problems with this (even adults!). In this chapter we'll look at how to get organized and plan better, in and out of school. We'll take a look at

• Getting organized
• Managing time
• Planning your goals

Getting Organized

If you're one of those students who finds last month's math homework on the bottom of your locker, buried under the sneaker you've been looking for since your PE teacher told you not to come back until you have two sneakers, you may need some help organizing. It may also be hard for you to keep track of school assignments and after-school activities.

Let's talk about how to get organized at home and at school.

Tips for Home

When you are organized at home, you feel better, spend less time looking for lost things, and make better use of your time. Here are ideas that have worked for other kids.

• Hang a large calendar in your bedroom. Write down reports, projects, tests, and special activities that are coming up. Each night, look at the next 3 days on your calendar so you know what to expect.

- Write yourself notes and put them where you will see them so that you remember important things to do.
- Use a shelf in your room just for books and papers for school.
- Find a place to keep long-term projects and important papers you are working on.
- Keep a family message board in the kitchen so that you and your family can leave reminder notes about events, appointments, and other important things.
    - Empty and organize your backpack every week. Try to do this on the same day every week.
    - Clean out your notebooks each week. Throw out papers that you do not need. Put all papers in their correct subject section. If you're not sure you need a paper, ask the teacher.
    - Pack your backpack at night, with all notebooks and homework inside, so you do not need to rush in the morning.

Getting organized takes work. But think of all that time you usually spend looking for lost stuff! Wouldn't it be great to spend time doing something fun instead?

Tips for School

Seems like teachers always talk about the importance of being organized. You can be sure they know what they're saying. Here are some suggestions worth trying:

- When you pack up each day, use a few minutes to make sure that you have all the homework materials and books you will need that day.
- Organize your school desk and locker each week.
- Use a homework assignment book. Before leaving school each day,

stop and check that homework is filled in for each subject. If there is no homework in a subject, write "none" or put X in the space.

• Always put important things in the same place in your backpack, locker, and desk.

• As soon as you get a paper from the teacher, put it in the correct folder or notebook section.

Once you feel organized at home and school, you can start walking around feeling pretty good. Parents and teachers may start to look at you in pleased amazement!

Managing Your Time

Part of being organized is managing your time. Time is funny. Have you ever noticed how quickly it goes when you're having a great time and how s-l-o-w even a few minutes can feel when you're bored? The point of good time management is to use time well. One way to manage your

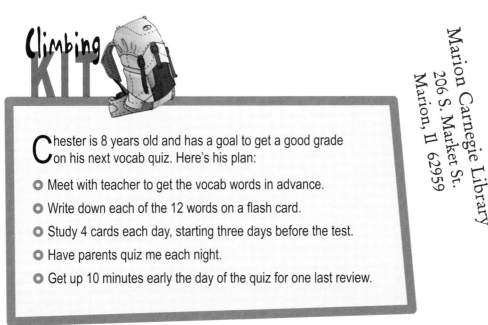

Chester is 8 years old and has a goal to get a good grade on his next vocab quiz. Here's his plan:

○ Meet with teacher to get the vocab words in advance.

○ Write down each of the 12 words on a flash card.

○ Study 4 cards each day, starting three days before the test.

○ Have parents quiz me each night.

○ Get up 10 minutes early the day of the quiz for one last review.

time is to learn to plan ahead. It saves a lot of work later! Here are some planning ahead tips:

- Try doing things in a logical order. For example, if you will be cooking something from a recipe, check the ingredients you will need **before** you begin cooking.
- When you have a big project or report, break it into small steps. Try finishing one or two steps each day.
- If there is a day when you will be busy after school (because of a dance recital or sports event), try to get your work done ahead of time.
- If it's hard for you to work for a long time, break big assignments or chores into smaller chunks of time. So if you have to clean your room, work hard for 15 minutes, take a break, work hard for 15 minutes, and take a break.
- Some people work better at different times of the day. Find out which is your "good time." and do the things that are hard for you at your "best" times.
- Wear a watch to remind you when to be somewhere.
- Use a timer, like a kitchen timer, to stay on track during homework.
- Use an alarm clock to wake yourself up for school.
- Write an after-school schedule for yourself. Include assignments, studying, chores and other things you need to do.

Learning to pay attention to time can take awhile to learn. Ask people who are good at it (a parent, tutor, or teacher) to help you get better at your own time-management skills.

Planning Your Goals

A goal is something you haven't done yet, but want to do. Our dog has always had a goal to catch a squirrel. He hasn't done it yet, but he keeps trying. How realistic is that? On the other hand, he has figured out how to reach his goal of getting treats by doing a rolling-over trick. He's good at that!

Setting goals gives you something to work toward. If you set out to climb a mountain—reaching the top is your goal. But do you go straight from the base of the mountain to the top? Well, unless you can fly, that's probably not possible.

- You take small steps to get to the top.
- You set a goal to reach a near point on the mountain.
- You get there, take a rest, and then go a little farther to another near point.

Climbing KIT

Measure Time

How can you learn how long things take? Practice! Try this with a homework assignment:

- ○ Write down how long you think one subject will take.
- ○ Look at the clock and begin.
- ○ When you're finished, check the clock and write down how long it took.

Do the times match? If there is a big difference, figure out why. The more you do this, the better you get at estimating how much time you **really** need for assignments. It's fine to ask an adult to help you with estimating time you'll need when it's a different kind of assignment.

Set realistic goals for yourself! Once you have set a goal, figure out the steps you need to take to get there.

• Talk with your teachers and parents about your goals.

• Think of simple goals you can handle.

• Remember to look for your own improvement without comparing yourself to your classmates. Your own improvement is the best measure of success!

If your goal is to do well on math tests, organize your studying and your time to reach that goal! If your goal is to learn how to do pottery, you may take a class and spend lots of time practicing. Having goals allows you to organize your thoughts and your tasks.

Well, it's true that it's not always easy to stay organized. But the more you try, the more in control you are. It's a good feeling!

In the next chapter, we'll look at technology and how it helps you with organization and school skills.

CHAPTER 8

Technology to the Rescue

Technology is a big help for people. It is especially helpful if you have LD! If you want to know how much technology has changed our world, talk to your grandparents or an older neighbor. Ask them what life was like before computers and cell phones. It was sure different! We will explain how technology (computers, software, small gadgets) can help you deal with your LD.

Computers and Laptops

When was the last time you used a computer? Maybe today? You know that computers help make reading, writing, and spelling easier! They also help you organize your ideas and time more easily. Computers are great because you are the boss. A computer doesn't yell when you make mistakes, and it helps fix your spelling errors. It follow your directions. You tell it when to start and when to stop. You can use them for word processing, studying, scheduling, and organization.

Keyboarding

A computer is easier and faster to use if you know where all the letters and numbers on the keyboard are without looking at them. Learning to keyboard can be helpful if you have poor handwriting or write slowly. You can keyboard at your own pace and your hand doesn't get tired. There are many software programs that teach you how to keyboard.

Help! I Forgot to Save My Work!

Don't let this happen to you! Remember:

- When you do work on the computer, stop often and save it.

- Print a copy of your homework in case you can't get to the computer later or something goes wrong when you save the file.

- Create a back-up file. Get your own flash drive and save your work on it. Bring it to school when you need it.

Word Processing

You can use word processing programs to take notes in class and write essays. With the push of a key, you can fix mistakes. Word processing programs check your spelling and grammar. (Unless your grandma likes to check your grammar!) Work done on word processors is neat and easy to read. Kids usually write more this way because it's faster to get ideas down.

We know a fourth grader whose handwriting was difficult to read. He really wanted a pet, so he wrote a beautiful essay using his computer and left it on the table for his parents to read. Well, they didn't get him a monkey, but they were so impressed by how much his keyboarding skills improved that they took him to the zoo to visit some monkeys!

Scheduling and Organization

Organization programs help you to keep track of assignments, due dates, and activities. You can find these programs on your computer, online, or on your PDA or smart phone. Use these programs to

- Write down chores, reminders, due dates, or assignments and check them off when you finish each one.
- Make a test studying schedule.
- Keep track of your activities and sports schedules.
- Write down people's birthdays.

Studying

Use technology to help you study.

- Make up your own study guide when preparing for a test. Keyboarding the information into the computer may help you memorize better.
- Use a color font or the highlighting feature for the most important facts you want to remember.
- Make an audio-digital recording of facts and information. Listen to it over and over until you really know it.

Helpful Software

Because most kids are comfortable using computers, it's a great tool for learning. Have fun exploring different software to see what works for you. Here we describe some helpful software.

Word Prediction Software

Do you have a hard time spelling or writing? With word prediction software, you keyboard the first letters of a word, and it guesses words that might fit into your sentence and start with these letters. For example, if you keyboard "br", it might guess the word *brush* if that would fit in your sentence. If the correct word isn't shown, you keyboard the next letter. Usually, no more than three letters need to be keyboarded before the computer shows the word you want, spelled correctly. Pretty cool, huh?

More About Fonts

The look and style of letters on the screen are called fonts. A font can be changed to make it easier to read. If you like bigger, bolder letters when you read from the screen, set the computer to that style. Fonts like Verdana, Tahoma, and Arial are very clear and easier to read. When you print, good fonts to use are Georgia, Garamond, and Times New Roman. Ask your teachers what fonts you should use for assignments and reports.

Graphic Organizers

There is software that makes graphic organizers such as a web on the computer to help organize your ideas before you begin writing. You can then change your information into outline form and then to an organized paragraph.

Voice Recognition Applications

If you find it hard to write or keyboard what you want to say, a voice recognition application might be just right for you. It recognizes your voice, and writes your words as you say them. You don't have to keyboard anything!

Text Recognition Applications

When you need to do lots of copying and editing, text recognition applications can really be handy. Instead of keyboarding from a printed page, a scanner copies the page for you. Then you can make any changes you want.

Word Recognition Reading Technology

This technology scans and reads aloud printed material. This is great for kids who have trouble reading books by themselves. The computer does the reading. You listen while following the words highlighted on the screen.

Audio Books

If reading is hard for you, or if you read very slowly, listening to books instead of reading them might be right for you! These books are called audio books. Many libraries have them. Other places can send you recorded books, including textbooks. Check out the resources section for more information.

Math Applications

There are lots of math applications that help kids. You may want to try these:

- Many websites provide video teaching of how to do math skills.
- Gadgets, like your cell phone and MP3 player, might have calculators.
- You can load a calculator and other math applications to your PDA or smart phone.

Small Gadgets

It seems that the more gadgets can do, the smaller they get. There are many small devices that can now help at home and at school. Here are some that might work for you:

- Cameras that can read text to you! Instead of you scanning text into a computer, these devices take pictures of the text and read it aloud to you.
- There are different kinds of mice (not the ones that eat cheese) that can be used, with optical track balls that are different sizes so you can pick what works best for you.
- Digital book players play audio versions of books using human voices.
- An e-book is a book that you download from the Internet into your computer. (E-book readers let you read on screen the book you downloaded.) Just think, you can take your e-book on your laptop instead of carrying heavy school textbooks.

More small gadgets come out every year, so there will be more and more ways to help you! Check our resources section for more helpful small devices and other technology.

Technology is an important part of your mountain climbing tool kit. Find technology that works for you. Soon there will be even more technology we can't even imagine yet! In the next section of the book, we will talk about five different kinds of LD and what you can do if you have any of them.

PART 3

CLIMBING MY MOUNTAIN:
ME AND MY LD

CHAPTER 9
Reading LD

When you have reading LD you are not able to read as well as students your age and grade should be able to do. Although you may be smart and good in many things, your reading skills are not yet at grade level. Adults sometimes call reading LD *dyslexia*. If you have reading LD, you may have some or many of these:

- A hard time remembering the sounds of letters.
- Trouble sounding out words and blending sounds together to make words.
- Getting confused by words that look nearly the same. (If the word is *where*, you may read *were*, or you may read *burnt* as *burst*.)
- Changing the order of letters in words. (If the word is *fast*, you might read *fats*.)
- Difficulty recognizing words, even ones you have seen many times.
- Trouble understanding what you read, even if you can read the words correctly.
- Reading very slowly.

If you have reading LD, you probably want to improve your skills so that reading becomes easier for you. No matter what grade you are in, there are lots of things you can do to become a better reader.

Strategies for Reading LD

Your teachers, parents and tutor work with you on skills. Playing reading games is a fun way to get extra practice. You also become a better reader by reading more and learning many reading strategies. In this chapter, we'll list some. Try them and see which work for you.

Sounding Out Words

You can sound out words letter-by-letter or sound-by-sound, then slide the letter sounds together. Here are two examples.

- Look at the word *sun*.

  Say each sound (s–ŭ–n).

  Now slide those three sounds together to say the word.

- Sometimes one sound is made up of more than one letter.

  Look at the word *check*.

  This time there are still three sounds, although the word looks longer.

  Say the sounds (ch–ĕ–ck).

  Slide those three sounds together to say the word.

Using Sight Words

Sight words are words that you memorize as whole words, so you don't need to sound them out each time you see them. Here are some common sight words: *the, said, have, she, of, do*. The more sight words you know, the easier it is to read. You can practice reading sight words by using flash cards or making card games with sight words.

Reading Long Words

Don't get scared when you see long words! Here are some tips for reading them:

- Look for compound words, which are made up of two small words. What may look like a big, new word may really be made of two words you already know (snow / flake, sun / tan, basket / ball).
- Look for small words that you already know within a bigger word (*part*ner or *own*ership).

raindrop daytime

firefighter softball meatball

sunshine suitcase

- Try breaking words into syllables. Remember, each syllable has its own vowel sound. (*Metric* has two syllables: met / ric. *Kangaroo* has three syllables: kan / ga / roo.) Teachers can help you learn more about breaking words into syllables.

Figuring Out New Words

When you come across new words, you may feel like skipping them. But don't do that! There are lots of ways to figure out new words. Try some of these ideas.

Look for familiar prefixes (at the beginning of words) and suffixes (at the end of words). Sometimes, just by reading those, you can figure out most of the word. Look at the word *previewed*. If you take away the prefix (*pre–*) and the suffix (*–ed*), you see the word *view*. Now put the word back together (*previewed*) and read the whole thing.

Look at Words Carefully

Learn to look carefully at the *insides* of words, because words sometimes almost look like other ones.

- Which would you rather float in: a *ship* or a *shop*?
- Which would you rather eat: a *bear* or a *bean*?
- Which would you like as a pet: a *cat* or a *coat*?

Use the other words in the sentence as clues. When you see a new word, sometimes you can read the rest of the sentence to figure out what makes sense in the sentence. For example, if you were reading *I was late for my _____ game*, you might guess *soccer* if the word started with s and *tennis* if the word started with t.

Use "word families" or "word chunks" to help you figure out new words. Once you know the word chunk *-at*, you can easily learn to read *fat, chat, splat,* and *splatter*. Once you know the word chunk *–in*, you can figure out the words *fin, chin,* and *dinner*.

Building Your Vocabulary

Did you ever read a chapter that was full of new words? It was probably really hard to understand. Having a good vocabulary makes it easier to understand what you hear and read.

Before you begin reading, try this. Look through the pages for words you don't know. Use a dictionary (or another person) to find out what the words mean. Write down the words and their meanings. Keep them in front of you, and look at them while reading.

Here are more tips to build your vocabulary:

- Use index cards to write a new word on one side and the meaning on the other side. Keep these cards in a box and review them until you know them.
- Keep a "new word journal" for the meaning of new words you learn.
- If someone uses a new word you don't know, ask what it means. We all learn lots of new words that way.
- Read all kinds of books. That will introduce you to all kinds of words.

You may know many words, but that's just part of being a good reader. You have to understand what you read, too. Teachers call this "comprehension." Let's talk about that.

Understanding What You Read

Once it becomes easier to read each word, you can move on to reading sentences and paragraphs. We put words and ideas together to understand what we read. Kids with reading LD may have trouble understanding what they read, even when they can read all the words. There are many things you can do to improve your comprehension.

Know your purpose for reading. If you are reading for enjoyment only, you will read differently than if you are being asked to look for specific information. When you have reading questions to answer for an assignment, you read more slowly and carefully.

Look questions over before you begin reading, so you are ready when you find the information. Keep the questions and a pencil near you as you read, and write down the answer or the page on which you found it.

Mark important information. Use sticky notes to mark pages that have important information or new vocabulary words to check. Put a symbol (such as a star or check mark) in front of sentences you do not understand, so someone can explain it later.

Use highlighters if you are allowed to write on the paper or in the book. Highlight important words in directions. (Circle the noun in each sentence.) You can also highlight main ideas and important details in paragraphs.

"Talk" to yourself. As you read, try to figure out main ideas. Write down the most important idea from each page or speak it into an audio recorder. This will give you a good summary when you finish reading.

Ask yourself if what you are reading makes sense. If not, go back and read the section again. If it is still confusing, ask for help.

Keep track of important information. When reading, use a large index card as your bookmark. Keep notes on it of things you want to remember, such as names of characters and family connections. When the book has a long description of something, try drawing it so you can see it better in your mind—for example, the way a character looks, the design of a house, a family tree. If a subject is difficult for you, read chapters more than once. You'll find more meaning the second time around.

Use different kinds of books. Try using large-print books, if small font is hard to read or try audio books. Use your ears to help you read! It may make it easier for you to understand the book.

Practice, Practice, Practice

The more you read, the more new words you learn and the easier reading becomes. Start with books you find a little easy to build your confidence. Here are some other ways to practice reading skills:

- Read about things that interest you. Sports statistics, really strange facts, kids' magazines, joke books—anything you really like will hold your attention as you read and help you to get good reading practice.
- Listen to an audio book and read silently or aloud with the narrator (as you follow along with your eyes on the page).
- Read an easy book to a younger child.
- Go to websites that help you practice your reading while having fun.

If you have reading LD, there are many people around the world like you! More good news: Your teachers, parents and tutors can help you improve your reading. Technology, such as audio books, also makes reading easier. Once you become a better reader, you will have gained a wonderful power! Now, let's take a look at another kind of LD, called math LD.

Math LD

We use math skills all the time. We count, add, subtract, measure, tell time, and solve problems. When you're saving up money for new songs to download, you're using math. When you divide up cookies among your friends you're doing math. Even if it's not your best subject, there are many things you can do to improve your skills and have fun doing them. In this chapter, we'll talk about what math LD is and look at ways to help you learn math.

What Is Math LD?

Kids with math LD have a great deal of trouble learning and understanding math. Their math skills are not as strong as those of other kids in their grade. They may need a lot more time to learn math. They may not learn math the way the other kids in class do. Kids with math LD may need teachers to teach them in a different way, so that math is not so difficult for them. If you have math LD, you may have a few or many of the following problems:

• Needing lots of extra practice before you understand new math ideas.

• A tough time understanding how to solve math problems.

• Not learning math facts as quickly or easily as other kids your age.

• Difficulty memorizing. This makes it hard to remember math facts you've learned and remember how to do math operations.

• Trouble working on math problems, especially ones with several steps.

• Making careless mistakes because you work too quickly and make careless errors.

• Working very slowly when you do math.

Math teachers and tutors know many ways to make it easier to learn math. If you have any of the math problems above, we hope you'll try some of these suggestions.

Strategies for Math LD

Even if you have a hard time with math now, you can still improve your skills. Technology may make math easier for you. Remember, there's no one right way to do math.

Use Your Senses

When you solve hard math problems, use things you can see, touch, and move with your hands, like dried beans, blocks, or coins. Being able to move these things around may help you understand math problems better than just using paper and pencil.

You can also try drawing a picture for a hard problem, because thinking it out in your head can be more difficult.

Keep Repeating Math Facts

Learn your math facts by practicing them on the computer or listening to them on a CD, over and over. Repetition may be boring, but it has been shown that it is the best way to remember.

Concentrate only on one family of numbers at a time so you don't overload your brain with other facts until you're ready. Set aside a whole week to learn one math fact family. Here's an example:

$$
\begin{array}{ccccccc}
3 & 3 & 3 & 3 & 3 & 3 & 3 \\
\times\,1 & \times\,2 & \times\,3 & \times\,4 & \times\,5 & \times\,6 & \times\,7 \\
\hline
\end{array}
$$

Let Your Paper Help You

Having the right kind of paper can help you with your math.

- Use graph paper to keep numbers lined up in straight columns. Write one number in each box.
- Turn lined notebook paper to the side, and line up your numbers in the columns.
- Be neat! If your math paper is too crowded with examples, rewrite them on a clean sheet of paper, where you can spread out and be accurate.
- Cover all other examples on the page except the one you are working on. Then you won't get distracted by other numbers.

Use Tools and Games

You don't always have to use paper and pencil to learn math. Here are other ways to learn.

- Use a calculator to check your work.
- Make math flash cards to practice on your own.
- Play computer games that let you practice your math skills.
- Do you have a piggy bank? Count your money. It's a good way to practice addition and multiplication.

Doing Word Problems

Are word problems hard for you? Here are some ideas to try.

- Underline or highlight the key words that are being asked (example: Find the <u>sum</u>).

Climbing KIT

Draw to Solve

Making a picture of what a word problem says can make it easier for you to solve it. Try drawing these on a piece of paper.

1. Phoebe had 4 cookies. Her sister gave her 2 more. Her dog stole 1 and ate it. How many cookies were left?

2. Yi has 5 shelves in his room. Each shelf has 7 books. How many books are on the shelves?

3. Samantha started the school year with 10 pencils. She won 5 more in a math contest. 4 of them broke, so she threw those away. How many were left?

4. Dylan had 20 pieces of paper. His teacher told him to keep 2 pieces for himself, then give 3 other kids the remaining pieces in equal amounts. How many did he give each kid?

- Read the problem several times, or read it aloud so you understand better what to do. Make sure you can read all the words in the problem. If not, ask someone to help you out.
- Estimate your answer before you work out a problem. Look over your final answer. Is it similar to your estimate? If not, check the problem again.

Who Can Help?

There are people on your climbing team who can help you with your math LD.

If you are having trouble learning math facts, you might want to:

- Ask someone to help you practice.
- Listen to an audio music recording of math facts.

If you have trouble with math homework, try the first few examples together with a parent or tutor. You can also ask them to give you extra practice doing word problems. In some schools, kids with math difficulties may work in a small group with a teacher who gives them extra help. There are websites that give you practice with math. You can do these by yourself!

If learning math is hard for you, doing extra work and getting the help you need may help you feel much better about doing math. Practice and ask questions. Soon you will find that this is a subject that makes sense to you! In the next chapter, we will look at a different kind of LD, written language LD.

CHAPTER 11

Written Language LD

Anyone who has ever been to school will tell you that you have to do plenty of writing there, so having written language LD can be tough! Many kids with written language LD have good ideas and lots of information in their heads. But it may be hard for them to write so others can understand it. Their ideas may not be organized or complete. They may make many mistakes in their written work. Writing may be much harder for them than speaking.

In this chapter, we'll talk about what exactly written language LD is. We'll also look at strategies to try.

What Is Written Language LD?

If you have a written language LD, you have a hard time putting your ideas on paper. You may also have poor handwriting and spelling. Writing assignments often don't show what you really know. If you have a written language LD, you may have a few or many of the following problems:

- Trouble putting your ideas in writing (even though you can talk about them well).
- Difficulty organizing your ideas when you write.
- A hard time putting your thoughts on paper so that others understand.
- Trouble using correct grammar and spelling when you write.
- Trouble writing clear, neat letters.
- Often erasing what you have written.
- Making many errors, like not using capital letters, correct punctuation, or complete sentences when you write.

Strategies for Written Language LD

If you have problems with written language, don't get frustrated! There are lots of strategies to improve your writing skills. Try these out and see which ones work for you.

- Try using cursive writing. It may be easier for you than printing because the letters flow into each other.
- Keyboarding may be easier for you to do than handwriting.
- Try skipping lines when you write or keyboard, so your work is easier to read and correct.
- Erasable pens make it easy to make corrections.
- Use very smooth pens or rubber pencil grips. Your hand may feel less tired.
- If you hold your pen or pencil too tightly, have someone teach you how to hold it correctly.

Organizing Your Writing

Here is something to try if you have a hard time organizing what you want to write.

Webs or mind maps can help you organize your ideas before you start your work. You can then use this information to form a paragraph. Here is an example of a web:

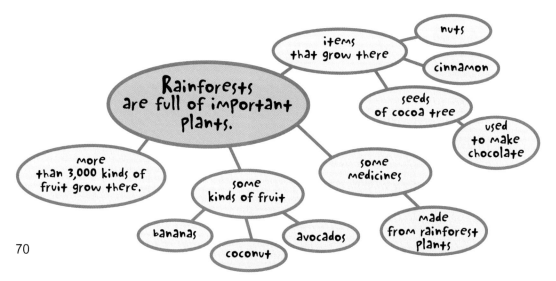

Here is a paragraph written using part of the web on the last page:

The rainforests of the world are full of important plants. There are more than 3,000 kinds of fruits that grow in the rainforest, including bananas, coconuts, and avocados. Seeds of the cocoa tree that are used to make chocolate, as well as cinnamon and nuts, are found in rainforests. Did you know that there are medicines made from rainforest plants? The rainforest is home to many important and useful plants.

Here are other ways to get organized before you start writing.

- Dictate your ideas to someone first or say them into an audio recorder.
- Use simple outlines to help you get organized before writing a paragraph or essay. (Remember, when you prepare a web or outline, you do not need to write full sentences, because this is just a quick way to put down your ideas.)

As you're organizing, remember that every paragraph should contain one main idea and sentences that give details about your main idea.

Climbing BREAK

Here's a sample outline of an essay about a fun trip!

A Big Adventure

I. Went camping last summer
  A. Three-day trip
    1. In the woods in Minnesota
    2. With my father and 2 cousins
    3. Slept in tents
    4. Went fishing at the lake
  B. Best parts
    1. Caught lots of fish
    2. Cooked and ate our meals outside
    3. Told ghost stories in the dark
  C. Worst parts
    1. Rained one night—got soaked
    2. Lost one of my shoes while hiking
    3. Two skunks also camped in our campsite!

Climbing KIT

Proofreading Your Work

Proofreading means looking over your work for mistakes. Here are some proofreading tips:

- Proofread your work once, walk away and come back later. You might find a few more mistakes!

- Make sure all your sentences are complete.

- Check that all punctuation is correct.

- Did you use capital letters correctly?

- Ask someone to help check your spelling or use spell-check on the computer.

Who Can Help?

Many people can help you become a better writer. Kids with written language LD often find it helpful to talk out their ideas with someone else before trying to write anything. That person can ask you questions that help you add more ideas. Teachers, tutors, and parents may work with you to organize your ideas and help fix mistakes.

If you have problems writing down what the teacher says, ask if a classmate can be a note-taker for you. Some teachers make a copy of another student's notes, so that you can have your own set to take home.

Who is the most important member of your team for written language LD? You guessed it: YOU. No one else has your ideas and your way of saying what you want to say. By the way, know one way to become a better writer? Read work that other people have written (like your classmates' work, newspapers, magazines, and books) and you'll find out that there are many good ways to write!

Writing well is hard to do for many people. Even some famous writers have admitted that writing was hard work for them, too! Here are quotes from two very important writers. What do you think they're trying to say?

"I'm not a very good writer, but I'm an excellent rewriter." —James Michener

"The wastebasket is a writer's best friend."   —Isaac Bashevis Singer

In the next chapter, we'll look at another kind of LD called oral language LD.

CHAPTER 12

Oral Language LD

Wouldn't the world be boring if everyone was too quiet? Talking and listening to each other are an important part of each day. We tell people what we think and what we need. We listen to conversations, to jokes, and to directions. But if using language is hard for you, all of these can be tough, and extra help may be useful In this chapter, we'll talk about what oral language LD is and look at strategies you can use if you have it.

What Is Oral Language LD?

You might be smart in many ways. But if you have a language disability, it may be hard for people to understand what you want to say. You may have difficulty deciding which words and sentences to use when you speak or putting your smart thoughts into words when you want to say something.

You may have a hard time understanding what other people say to you, especially when they speak quickly or use complicated sentences. It may be hard to understand what you read, even if you can sound out all the words correctly. Let's take a look at language problems and then some helpful strategies you can use. You may have trouble:

• finding the right words when you are talking;
• learning and using new vocabulary;
• organizing your ideas so they make sense;
• understanding and following spoken directions, especially when they have many steps;

- speaking clearly so that others can understand your words;
- using correct grammar;
- understanding when other kids say something funny or tell a joke;
- listening and understanding when someone talks; or
- entering or leaving a conversation or speaking in a group discussion; You may interrupt other people's conversations because you are not sure when it is your turn to speak. You may talk on and on without getting to the point.

Talking About and Explaining What You Mean

These ideas might work for you.

Hold on to what you want to say. Write down your ideas if you have something you want to remember so you won't lose your thought. Write in your notebook or on a sticky note and attach it to your notebook or desk.

Get your ideas across. Try starting your sentence by saying what your subject is (my baseball game, my friend's broken leg). Your ideas will follow more easily. Focus on getting your idea across, not on coming up with the exact word.

Practice. Practice by talking to yourself in front of a mirror. Work with your parents, too. They can listen to you while you practice saying what you would like to tell someone. For example, practice letting your coach know what helps you during softball games or telling your brother why you don't want him to borrow your clothes.

Climbing KIT

More Tips for Speaking in Class

If it's hard for you to speak in class, try these:

- Ask your teacher to tell you ahead of time when it will be your turn to speak.
- Take your time. Before you answer a question, say, "Let me think."
- Take time to picture your answer or ideas in your mind. Then try to describe them, using your picture.
- Organize some notes in writing before you speak in front of a group.

Have conversations with people who make you feel comfortable (like your grandpa who thinks you are brilliant or your babysitter who loves to talk sports with you). The more you practice speaking, the better you'll get!

Understanding What You Read

Sometimes difficulty understanding language makes it hard to understand what you read. Chapter 9 gives you some important tips for this. For example:

- Know your purpose for reading.
- Mark important information.
- Talk to yourself to figure out what the main idea is.
- Use audio or large print books.

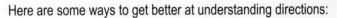

Understand Directions

Here are some ways to get better at understanding directions:

If you don't get the teacher's directions, work out a plan for a classmate to explain them to you a second time before you start your work.

- Ask your teacher or parents to give you simpler written directions that are broken down into smaller chunks whenever possible.

- Ask fast-talking people to please slow down when speaking.

- Quietly repeat directions to yourself before you follow them. This will help you to remember them.

Understanding What You Hear

When you listen to people speak, do you get confused by what they said? After your teachers give directions, do you still not know what to do? If understanding what you hear is hard, give some of these a try:

Speak up if you don't "get it". Let people know if you didn't understand what they said completely. Ask the person to explain it in a different way or to use drawings if that helps you.

Use audio recorders. If you know that your teacher will be talking about something important in class, find out if you can audio record it. Listen to the recording later as many times as you want

Try this at home, too: Your parents could record what you need to pack for an overnight trip or how to do a chore.

Draw to understand. When someone says something that is confusing to you, draw cartoons or simple pictures to help you understand. For example, if your math teacher tells you to fold a paper into 8 boxes and put your name in the top right box, try drawing this first to make sure you understand. This works with directions at home, too.

Listen. When someone is talking to you, look at the person. This will help you understand better. When you are talking or listening, turn down distracting background noise (like the TV).

Climbing
BREAK

Did you know? "Variable speed control tape recorders" allow you to listen to the recorder and slow it down or speed it up. This gives you a chance to listen as many times as you want, at a speed that works for you!

Talking With Other People

Talking to adults and friends is important. You need to be able to explain why you need permission to leave your class or ask a friend if he wants to come to your house. These ideas that follow may help you be better understood by others.

Be polite. When someone is speaking to you, or you are talking to someone, look at the person. Wait until the other person finishes speaking before you begin talking. Make sure to give other people a chance to speak.

Learn how to join a group conversation. When you approach a group of people, listen for at least 20 seconds to figure out what everyone is talking about. Think about what you will say. Then talk if what you want to say is on the topic they are talking about.

Take your time. Don't rush what you are trying to say. Give yourself extra time to speak until you get your ideas out.

Who Can Help?

When people climb a mountain, it is important for them to talk to each other and help each other climb. If you cannot understand someone, stop and figure out how to communicate better. When you have an oral language LD, your team members will give you good advice.

- A speech-language pathologist can show you ways to improve language skills, because he or she has special training in working with people who need language help.
- Teachers help by making sure you understand directions and giving you extra time to think about what you want to say before you speak in class.

Parents help by:

- Giving you the time you need to figure out what you want to say.
- Teaching you the meaning of new words.
- Reminding you to make eye contact when you are talking or listening to someone.

We speak and listen every day. If either one of these is hard for you, you will need extra help to make school easier. Luckily, there are many ways that you can get this kind of help. Once you learn to use language well, many things will start to feel easier. In the next chapter, we'll take a look at a different kind of LD, called Non-Verbal LD.

CHAPTER 13
Non-Verbal LD

n this chapter we will describe what it means to have a non-verbal LD (also called NLD) and talk about what you can do to improve your skills. Kids with non-verbal LD have many good learning skills, like a strong vocabulary and good spelling. But it may be hard for them to do some kinds of writing. They may also have other problems. We'll look at strategies to try if you have NLD.

What Is Non-Verbal LD?

Non-Verbal LD (NLD) is when the brain has trouble understanding information that does not use words, like a photograph or a map. NLD is different from other LDs that we have talked about. It does not have to do with any one school subject. It can affect any part of school and home life. Kids with NLD have important strengths. For example, they may be good at paying attention to details and at using words and may be great talkers!

Signs of NLD

If you have NLD, you might have problems in one or more areas. Some kids with NLD have difficulties remembering things they have seen. Some have difficulty understanding when people use their face or body to show their feelings. Some kids with NLD have a hard time with their sense of balance and physical activity.

In the next sections, we'll talk about specific NLD problems. These may include difficulties with:

- Reading and math
- Being flexible (able to "go with the flow")
- Physical activities and handwriting
- Understanding feelings
- Getting along with others

Let's look at these challenges and strategies to overcome them.

Understanding Reading and Math

If you have NLD, you may be able to do math calculations and read words well, but you might still have trouble with:

- Understanding what a paragraph or story means. It may be hard to see (in your mind's eye) the different scenes in the book, and to understand main ideas.
- Understanding some math concepts, such as fractions and solving math problems.
- Writing out math examples in straight columns.

Climbing KIT

Checklist for Cleaning Your Bedroom

If jobs with lots of steps seem too much for you, try making a checklist. Here's one for cleaning your bedroom:

1. Put dirty clothes in the hamper.
2. Put all shoes on the floor of the closet.
3. Hang up anything that belongs in the closet.
4. Place all books on the bookshelf.
5. Make the bed.
6. Sweep the floor.
7. Throw away any trash.

Being Flexible

People are flexible if they are able to change quickly when necessary. For example, if you have NLD, you may be able to follow school rules well, but have a hard time if a rule or schedule suddenly changes. You might have:

- Difficulty getting used to tests or homework when they are set up in a new way. For example, if your teacher always gives multiple-choice tests and suddenly she gives a true/false test, it might be hard for you to make that switch.

- A hard time when the schedule at home or school changes.
- Trouble staying organized. For example, you don't like your new backpack because it does not have the same sections as the old one did.

Physical Activities and Handwriting

Isn't it annoying to be one of the last kids in your class to learn to ride a bike? Well, some kids with NLD have trouble with this or other kinds of activities that use the body. Here are some examples:

- You may sometimes be clumsy and have a hard time tying shoe laces or running well. We call these problems with motor coordination. You have trouble writing neatly, using scissors well, or doing art work, like drawing or painting.
- You might get lost easily and have difficulty finding your way around.
- You have trouble getting to classes or the school bus on time.
- You might be sensitive to loud noises or have sensitive skin (like having a tag in your shirt that bothers you).

Understanding Feelings

Excitement, pain, anger, sadness, and happiness are all feelings. Controlling your feelings is easier when you understand and can express them. But some kids with NLD have difficulties with feelings:

Climbing KIT

Practice using the muscles in your fingers and hands to make them stronger. This may help your handwriting. Try some of these:

- String beads.
- Learn to sew or knit.
- Play with Legos or small blocks.
- Glue pasta, rice, or dried beans on to paper.
- Pick up small items using tweezers.
- Learn to tie different kinds of knots.
- Use zippers.
- Play with clay.

• You may get very frustrated and have something adults call meltdowns. Meltdowns are when someone starts crying and yelling in frustration. It may upset other people when they see you act this way, especially if they can't figure out what is going on with you.

• You may not know how to talk about your feelings. Instead of talking about feelings, you would rather be left alone.

Getting Along With Others

One kid with NLD said to us, " School problems don't bother me so much. What really bothers me is not having friends." If you have NLD, you might have trouble getting along with other kids (socializing) because:

• You feel uncomfortable in new social situations, like parties or large groups.

• You spend too much time alone and might feel unhappy.

• You miss the point of a joke and think that when someone makes a joke, the person is being mean to you.

• You have trouble understanding behaviors or "reading faces" of people.

What can you do if you have these problems? Here are some ideas that have worked for kids with NLD.

Strategies for NLD

Just like there are many ways to learn, there are many ways to work with NLD and feel good about yourself. You may have already found some strategies earlier in the book that will help with reading, writing, and understanding math. You can also learn about dealing with your feelings in Chapter 15 and about making friends in Chapter 17. Be sure to check those out.

Being More Flexible

Many people have a hard time being flexible all the time. If this is often a problem, try these:

- Ask your parents and teachers to let you know when your usual routine will be changing, so you have a chance to ask questions and get ready before it happens.
- Keep a big calendar in your room and write down when something special is happening (such as a book report due date or your cousin coming to visit).
- Try walking to your classes with someone, so you don't have to worry about getting lost or being late.

Dealing With Noise

If noises bother you, try some of these ideas:

- If someone in your class has a voice that bothers you, talk to the teacher about giving you a seat away from that person.
- Use earphones during noisy activities.
- Ask your parents to make a quiet spot at home for when you need it.
- Try to be prepared ahead of time for loud noises like a school bell or fireworks. Then you won't be as surprised by it, and you can cover your ears.

Being Comfortable With Your Body

When your body feels good, you have more energy to do what you want. You may find some of these ideas helpful.

- Ask your parents to cut the tags out of your shirts so they don't bother you.
- Wear loose-fitting clothing and shoes that feel good.
- Exercise! Exercising makes your body stronger. It also helps work off any extra energy or frustrations you have.
- If you have difficulties with one sport, try another! Don't like running? How about swimming? Is gymnastics too hard? Try yoga for kids. Can't ride a bike? How about a hike!

Improving at School

- Talk to your teacher about having a "directions buddy" in your class. This is someone who can help you with directions when you don't know what you are supposed to do.
- Work with a parent, teacher or counselor to write a list of all the steps you need to do to finish a project. Then, it won't feel like too much for you. Check off each step as you complete it.
- Ask your teacher to let you know ahead of time what types of questions will be on the test so you know what to expect.

Who Can Help?

There are lots of people on your climbing team who can help with your NLD. They are like the good buddies who help a tired or thirsty person climb up the mountain. Some of these people may be on your team:

- An **occupational therapist** or a **physical therapist** helps kids use fingers, hands, and other parts of their body to do exercises and activities. They may also help if you don't like the feel of some things you touch.

- Your parents and teachers will help you with problems that come with NLD, such as difficulties in schools and understanding your feelings.
- A counselor or therapist can help you learn skills to understand and get along with other people. You may learn some new ways to relax and solve problems.
- If you play a sport, your coach may help you learn to be a better player and be a member of a team.

NLD is a special kind of LD that makes important things in life somewhat difficult, like getting along with others, participating in sports, and completing writing assignments. We hope you found useful suggestions in this chapter. Now we are ready to talk in the next section about how to make your life outside of school go well.

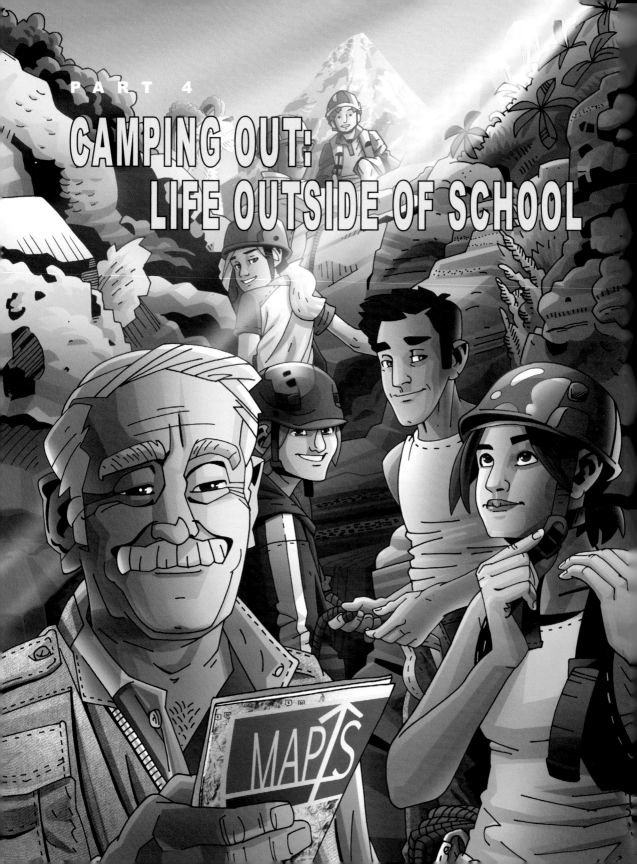

PART 4

CAMPING OUT:
LIFE OUTSIDE OF SCHOOL

CHAPTER 14

Making Home
Your Kind of Place

After a long day of carrying around a heavy backpack, writing until your hand hurts, and sitting too long in one place, it feels good to have a friendly, relaxed place to come back to. Home— a place to take a break, feel calm and recharge so you can do things later in a good mood.

We'll talk about ways to manage time at home, to set up your own personal space, and to get along with parents and siblings.

Improving Your Life at Home

How can I make my life at home better and more relaxing? We knew you would ask! We have ideas about what you can do in the morning, after school, at night, and on weekends.

In the Morning

A good morning usually leads into a good day. Get your morning off to a good start by doing these:

- Set up a morning routine, so tasks like brushing your teeth become almost automatic.
- Wake up early enough so you have time to do everything slowly.
- Eat breakfast by yourself if you like quiet.
- Have breakfast together with someone in your family who makes you happy.

Climbing KIT

Manuel's No-Rush Plan

Manuel always rushed around each morning, and sometimes missed his school bus. "Enough of this!" he finally said, and decided to try something different. Here is his plan.

Night before	Morning
Pack backpack.	Wake up.
Put out clothes for next day.	Get dressed.
Pour cereal into a bowl and cover for breakfast tomorrow.	Pack lunch and snack.
	Add milk to cereal, pour juice.
Set alarm clock.	Eat breakfast.
Shower.	Brush teeth.
Brush teeth.	Take backpack.
Good night!	Leave, smiling and on time!

After School

Some stress at school comes from the hard work you do. So when it's time to relax at home, do things that make you happy.

- Get outside! Being in your backyard or a park are fun and give a feeling of peace.
- Exercise. Run outside, bike, or go for a walk.
- Pay attention to nature. When some kids do homework outdoors, they concentrate better.
- Unplug yourself! Turn off the TV, computer, or MP3 player. At first, it might be difficult, but do this for part of each day. It's hard to relax when you are always "plugged-in."
- Keep up with friends. Invite kids to hang out with you.

In the Evening

Once homework is done, it's time to relax. Here are some ideas for winding down before it's time to go to sleep.

- Take a relaxing shower.
- Pack up everything you'll need for school the next day. Put it in the same place every night.
- Listen to music or a story before going to sleep.

Setting Up Your Space

No matter what size your home is, it's good to have a personal spot that feels special to you. It may be a cozy corner or your own room. It can be a place to read, listen to music or just think. Use your imagination to set it up.

- Create a corner with pillows, favorite books, a poster, or a CD collection.
- Talk to your parents about getting a comfortable chair, a desk, or a shelf to store hobbies.

Create your own homework spot.

- Find a place without distractions.
- Keep it organized so homework and projects don't disappear.
- Store supplies there that you need for homework (extra paper, ruler, erasers).

Climbing BREAK

Respect Your Body

Feeling good makes it easier to learn. Remember to:

- Eat healthy meals. (Don't forget breakfast.)
- Get enough sleep.
- Exercise often.
- Be with friends.
- Talk to an adult if something is bothering you.

Dealing With Your Family

Some homes and families are quiet and organized, and others are noisy and busy. Whatever your home is like, it can be a special and fun place. Let's look at ways for you and your family to make home great.

Parents

Your parents know you really well. They usually know what works for you, what makes you happy or angry. They are the part of your climbing team that has been with you the longest. They'll stick by you when the mountain feels hard to climb and help you! Ask for help or advice when you need it. But, to become an independent person, try to also find ways to manage some situations on your own.

• Decide together how much free time you get each day. You deserve time to hang out or play. Prove to your parents that once you do begin your homework, you will finish it.

• Plan a time each evening when it will be quiet at home. Some families set a time every day when the television is turned off. This makes it easier to get homework done.

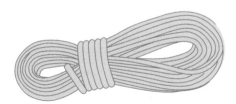

• Schedule 30 minutes each afternoon or evening when a parent is available to help you with school and non-school stuff.

• When your parents give you directions, ask them to write them down or record them. You won't have to try to remember everything later, and they won't feel that you ignored them.

• Talk with your parents about those times when you can manage problems on your own and times when you want them to "fight your battles" for you. (If you received a grade you thought was unfair, do you need a parent to talk to the teacher or can you discuss it yourself?)

• Make time to do fun things with family members. Do you like to play tag with your sister? Cook with your dad? Beat your aunt at chess?

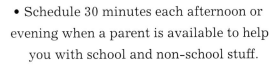

Climbing BREAK

Ideas for Good Communication at Home

Here are some ways to communicate with your family:

- Message board
- Family meetings
- Family calendar
- Chore wheel
- Family dinners

How does your family communicate?

Siblings

Living with brothers and sisters (siblings) can sometimes be pretty fun, but not always. The good news is that many brothers and sisters grow up to become good friends. Why not start now to get along well together? Think about these suggestions:

- Don't compare yourself to a brother or sister. Things that they do easily may not be easy for you, but you probably do other things better than they do.
- Ask your parents to make clear rules that will make it harder for your siblings to annoy you.
- Put labels on your special toys, so siblings don't take them away.
- Ignore annoying behavior. Sometimes a sibling does something just to see you react.
- Try the loving approach. Do things for siblings like bringing them things they need and helping them find something they misplaced.
- Tell your siblings when they're bugging you. If they don't know what upsets you, they can't stop doing it.

Your day at school is very important. So is your day after school. Make yourself a comfortable space at home, learn to enjoy being with family and friends, and take good care of yourself. All these can make after-school time and weekends a happy part of your life. In the next chapter, we'll take a look at a very important part of you—your feelings.

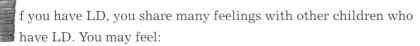

CHAPTER 15

Dealing With Feelings

f you have LD, you share many feelings with other children who have LD. You may feel:

- **frustrated** when you work hard but still don't get the right answers and good grades;
- **angry** when you don't understand what some kids already know;
- **sad** if what you know in your head gets jumbled up when you try to say it or write it;
- **unsure** of yourself when your progress is slow or comes only in small steps; or
- **worried** when you take a test because you're afraid you won't know the answers.

You're not alone in feeling sad or angry or anxious. Other kids also have these feelings. Let's talk about these feelings and what you can do about them.

Frustration

Life is full of fun stuff that feels easy to do. For kids with LD, it's hard to do some things, like learning, so school may not always feel fun. Let's face it, even if learning is hard, we still need to know how to read, write, and do math. We use these skills at school and in jobs when we grow up.

When something feels difficult, you may become frustrated, impatient, and tired. These feelings are normal. Here are some things you can do when you feel frustrated:

- Take a deep breath. Relax your hands and arms.
- Put your hands behind your head and stretch.
- Take a break when something feels hard. Do something different for a few minutes.
- When you have a lot of work, take a small step to get started.

Anger

Anger is what you feel when you are very frustrated. You may feel angry when you try to study or do homework as best as you can, and still nothing goes right. When you get angry, you might start feeling fidgety and hot, your heart might beat faster, and you might clench your teeth and fists. Everyone feels angry sometimes. It's all right to feel angry. But too much anger can be harmful, so it's good to take control of it. Try some tips to help manage your anger without hurting yourself and other people.

- Remove yourself from other people when you know that you are angry, so you don't say or do things you may later regret.
  - At home, go to your room to calm down.
  - Punch a pillow or punching bag.
  - Draw a picture that shows how you feel.
  - Be active. With your parent's permission, run around the block, or ride your bike. Play extra hard at recess.
    - Make a list of complaints. Make it as long as you want!
    - When you calm down, talk about your complaints with your parents, teacher, or counselor.

Sadness

Sadness is when you feel like crying. What many kids don't realize is that sadness can come with frustration and anger. If you are frustrated, you might feel sad when you think that there is nothing you can do to feel better. Getting poor grades or being teased at school can also make you feel sad. To help yourself feel less sad:

• Remind yourself who loves you—parents, relatives, and friends.
• Play with your pet.
• Talk with a friend.
• Create a playlist of your favorite music and songs and listen to them.
• Make your own book of jokes and riddles that make you laugh and read it.
• Make a list of 10 things that make you happy.

Climbing BREAK

Your Relaxation Trip

Feeling anxious? Take a relaxation trip in your head. Try to focus on a favorite place, like a hike in the mountains. Think about:

○ Tall, shady trees all about you.
○ Birds chirping.
○ The cool breeze on you cheeks.

○ The warm sun on your back.
○ The place ahead of you where you will rest, drink water, and look down the mountain.
○ Deer drinking at a stream!
○ Fields and meadows full of sweet smelling flowers.

Anxiety

Anxiety is another word for feeling very worried. Everyone feels anxiety at times. It is hard to learn and worry at the same time. Anxiety is one reason why some kids with LD don't like school and homework. If you are worried about something, it may be hard to pay enough attention to learning. Often, when the problem improves, you'll feel better and have less trouble learning. In the meantime you can try some of these suggestions:

- Close your eyes. In your mind, take a relaxation trip and picture a favorite place.
- Exercise! Dance. Run. Moving your body can help calm anxious feelings.
- Write down a plan when you feel like you have too much to do.
- Think about what is bothering you and talk about it with your parents or counselor.
- Take deep breaths and relax your muscles.

In this chapter we talked about feelings that sometimes get in your way. But let's not forget that you have the power to take control over these feelings. With a little effort, you can make room for all the good feelings to shine through, like pride, excitement, and happiness! In the next chapter, we'll look at a very important feeling—how you feel about yourself.

CHAPTER 16

Feeling Good About Yourself

Wouldn't it be nice to always feel good about yourself? Yes! Do most people always feel that way? No! Do people with LD sometimes feel badly about their learning problems? Yes! Some kids with LD spend too much time thinking badly about themselves. Not a good idea! Feeling good about yourself gives you energy and excitement to try hard at things. When you believe in yourself, you feel you can do many things. Let's take a look at what you can do to feel good about yourself.

Accept Your Strengths and Weaknesses

When you have LD, you may say, "Why me? It's not fair." But this is like saying, "Why am I so tall?" or "It's not fair that I have straight hair." Remember, this is who you are, different from others in some ways and like them in some ways. Just like you, everyone is special and different from others. When you accept that the world is wonderful because people are each so different, you will like yourself even more, along with your own strengths and weaknesses.

Accepting your strengths and weaknesses lets you be proud of yourself. How should you begin? First, don't turn this page until you can say three really good things about yourself! Next, try some of these ideas:

• Laugh at yourself and don't be afraid of making mistakes.
• Learn to accept criticism and make good use of it. Think about how you can use it to help improve what you're doing.

Climbing BREAK

Helping others makes you feel proud of yourself. Here are some things to try:

- Read to a younger brother, sister, or neighbor.
- Bring food to a homeless shelter with your family.
- Volunteer to take care of someone's pet.
- Help your parent or grandparent in their home.
- Visit someone who lives in a nursing home.
- Join a fundraising event for a charity.
- Give compliments. Watch people smile.

• Make a list of all the good things you know about yourself. Include good things your parents, teachers, and friends have told you. Remembering what they said will help you appreciate yourself even more.

• Help others. We all can do nice things for others. It makes us feel warm inside. Try it. You will see that you have something important to offer other people.

Use Self-Talk

Self-talk is having a conversation inside your head. You talk to yourself to find ways to solve problems and encourage yourself. It means being a good friend to yourself. Think of it as your own pep talk! Here are some ways to use self-talk:

- Give yourself compliments. Tell yourself how you have improved. For example, you could say, "I was only 5 minutes late for class instead of 10 this time."
- Remind yourself that work does not need to be perfect to show improvement. Sometimes just trying hard deserves a "good for me," no matter how it turns out.
- Talk to yourself positively. Encourage yourself. When you start thinking you did not do well on an assignment, ask yourself how you can improve next time.
- Remind yourself of the people who are there to help you. You have a strong climbing team to support you when you need them.

- Tell yourself that almost everything can improve if you stick to it and try and try again.
- If you try hard and something still doesn't work, use self-talk to have courage to accept and understand that failures are only a small part of life.
- Remind yourself of all the other things that can make you happy now. Your LD is only one part of your life.
- Tell yourself that this LD seems big now, but as you grow up, you learn to manage it. Things change and you will learn to overcome many challenges.

Use self-talk to encourage yourself, to compliment yourself, and to remember all of your great qualities.

Climbing KIT

Examples of Positive Self-Talk

Learn how to talk to give yourself a pep talk. Here's what some kids say:

- Isabel says, "I have trouble reading, but my artwork is great."

- Chen says, "I wish I was better in math, but I'm proud of the poems I write."

- Juan says, "I have LD in writing, but I'm an A math student!"

- Mac says, "I'm not too good in soccer, but I'm great at swimming."

- Ms. Roberts, a fifth-grade teacher says, "What I like most about teaching kids with LD is that they are willing to try hard and don't feel sorry for themselves. They keep going until they find something that works."

Develop Your Strengths

Building up your strengths is a great way to become more self-confident. If you're good in gymnastics, work hard on the balance beam or parallel bars. If you're good at art, work at drawing and painting. Remember, the world can use good gymnasts, talented gym teachers, artists, and illustrators!

What if you don't know yet what your strengths are? Here are some ideas:

• Try new things and activities you enjoy. This gives you a chance to learn about yourself.
• Look over old report cards with your parents. See what your teachers thought you were good at.
• Work with a social worker, psychologist, or counselor to help you find your strengths and feel good about yourself.

Learn From Your Mistakes and Failures

When something works for you, keep doing it. If it doesn't work, it may not be right for you. But before you throw away an idea or stop trying something that's hard, figure out why it wasn't successful. Remember that everyone makes mistakes. That is often the way we get better at something. Everyone can learn from their failures and mistakes. Here is what one student did to learn from his mistakes.

A sixth grader studied for a big social studies test by making note cards. He got a poor grade on the test. Instead of saying, "I'll never study that way again!" he talked it over with his tutor. They decided that he studied too many cards each day, and waited until late each evening to begin studying. Together they worked out a plan to help him study smarter next time. Instead of thinking he was bad at studying, he used the problem to learn something new about himself.

A seventh grader skipped the whole last page of questions on her math page. She was surprised that she was the first one to finish the test, but didn't stop to check her work. Thinking about her mistakes later, she decided to make two changes. The first was not to be afraid to ask her teacher when something seemed strange to her. The second was to always look back at each example on the test paper before she handed it in. She learned from her mistakes and felt great that she knew she would never make those mistakes again.

Got problems? Made a mistake? Do something about it. Solved the problem and learned from your mistake? That should feel pretty good!

Friends

Good friends know you well, like you and help you feel good about yourself. To get support from friends, here's what you can do:

- Hang around people who are nice to each other. If they aren't, they are not good friends. Say goodbye to them.
- Look for people who have some of the same interests you have. When you get together you will have fun. Or try something new your friend likes, and then have him/her try something you like.

We'll talk more about making and keeping friends in the next chapter.

Activities and Hobbies

If learning is hard for you, it's important to do things you like when school is over. Activities and hobbies give us a chance to learn more about ourselves and have fun. When you do what you love, you improve the way you feel about yourself.

Want to try something new that you might enjoy? What about these?

• Karate
• Drawing and painting
• Music
• Dance
• Acting
• Chess
• Origami
• Cooking

Think of a hobby you might like. You never know what you're good at until you try it.

Let's review. Talk to yourself in positive ways. Find friends who are fun to be with. Get involved in activities you enjoy. Remind yourself that it is all right to make mistakes, especially when you learn from them. Most of all, remember you are a great person, despite your weaknesses and with all your strengths.

In the next chapter, we'll look at people on your team who help you feel good— your friends.

CHAPTER 17

Making and Keeping Friends

Many kids have good friends, but some don't, even though they want friends. Sometimes other kids don't understand LD very well and make fun of kids who have it. That makes it hard for some kids with LD to make and keep friends.

There are many ways to make and keep friends. In this chapter, we'll talk about how to reach out to other kids. First, let's talk about reasons you might have trouble making and keeping friends.

Problems Making Friends

Do any of these look familiar?

- You might be very sensitive to what other kids say and do. It's easy to make a mistake and think something happened that really didn't. For example, one of your friends begins to talk to someone you don't like. That doesn't mean he stops being your friend.

- You may have trouble figuring out how people are feeling by looking at the expressions on their faces or listening to their words. For example, you think your soccer teammates are angry with you because they're telling you to try harder. But if you look carefully at their faces and listen, you'll see that they were really trying to encourage you to do your best.

- You may have difficulty listening to and understanding directions. For example, your best friend may have asked you to do something, but you didn't understand all the directions and did it wrong.

- You may find it frustrating to play games with rules. You may forget some rules and the other kids get upset.

If you have some of these problems, don't worry! You can learn to do something about them.

Making New Friends

Have you tried these?

- Think of someone you would like to spend time with.
- Try to find kids who have similar interests to yours.
  If you and a classmate both like Legos, invite him to your house to play.
- If you go to after-school activities, you may meet someone there you like.
- Get to know your friends' friends or the children of some of your parents' friends. You will have an advantage when playing with these kids because you already have a friend in common.
- Either on your own, or with the help of your parents, make plans to hang out with a new friend. Get together for an hour. If that goes well, next time get together for a longer time.
- Think up a few sentences that explain your LD, in case someone asks you about it. ("Kids with LD are smart. We just need to learn some school subjects differently. Millions of people have LD.")
- If it is hard for you to be in big groups of people, like birthday parties or group activities, ask your parents to first help you to get together with only one or two friends at a time.

Joining a Group

Joining large groups at parties, recess, and on the playground can be difficult. Things move so fast, and other kids may pay attention mostly to other friends in the group. Here is some advice to follow when you want to be part of a large group:

- Don't be discouraged if at first no one pays attention to you. It's normal for the old members of a group to ignore newcomers. Ask your parents about this. They'll probably tell you it's happened to them, too.
- Use a strong voice to say what you want, even if all you say is, "Can I join you?" Then, kids are more likely to respect you and make room for you. If you talk in a weak voice, the group may ignore you.
- Rehearse speaking in a strong voice with your friends or parents before you try to join a group. Practice introducing yourself, too.
- Join a group only if you have some things in common with kids in that group. Don't try to join a group playing Lacrosse if you are more of a football player and know nothing yet about Lacrosse.
- Be prepared. If you know what the group usually talks about, think of something to say ahead of time that you can add to the conversation.
- It's better to listen than to talk if you have nothing to add to the conversation.
- At first, talk about the same topic others talk about, and only when there is a break in the conversation. Try hard not to interrupt.
- If you want to be part of a recess game and can't find a group to join, look for kids who are not playing a game. Sometimes these kids will be happy to start a new game. Then you can help form a nice group of your own.

Being a Friend

Being a good friend takes work but it's worth it! Everyone can learn to be a good (or better) friend. Here are some ways to do it:

- Be loyal to your friends. Don't talking badly about them to others. Don't leave them out when you're with a group.
- Do nice things for friends. If books fall out of their book bag, help pick them up.

Climbing BREAK

Dos and Don'ts of Friendship

Don't	Do
Don't tease.	Do be friendly.
Don't interrupt others.	Do give others a chance to talk.
Don't be bossy.	Do make decisions together about what to play.
Don't let someone bully you.	Do tell your parent, teacher, or coach so they can help.

- Treat others the way you want to be treated.
- Learn to read faces and body language. Pay attention to how people look when you say or do something, so you can quickly fix mistakes if you said something wrong. Ask your parents or counselor to help you learn to do this.
- Be a good listener. Look people in the eyes. If people say something you don't understand, ask politely for another explanation.
- Apologize if you hurt a friend's feelings.
- Tell a friend to remind you of a rule if you forget it.
- Show other kids how you shine. Show things you do well, but don't brag!

Dealing With Teasing

Sometimes other kids can be pretty mean and tease you. It happens to lots of people, but it still hurts when it happens to you. What should you do if someone says something mean to you? Here are some ideas.

- Try ignoring it the first time. Just walk away.
- Try to keep a calm expression on your face so others don't see that you're bothered.

- Use humor. Sometimes, that takes away the other kid's power to hurt. Here are two examples of how you can respond.

> Bully: Why did you get that ugly haircut?
> You: I entered an ugly haircut contest and was the winner.

> Bully: How come you're always the last one to finish tests?
> You: It's my specialty.

- Practice saying something true when someone teases you about having LD. ("I go to the resource room so I can work in a quiet place with a helpful teacher.")
- If someone makes a mean comment about you in a group, laugh and say something like, "That goes for you, too." If the kids in the group see that you are not a "push-over" and that you can laugh at yourself, they are likely to respect you better.

Kids who bully or tease aren't your friends. Hang out with people who are fun and nice to you. Kids tend to pick on children who don't feel comfortable with themselves. Learn to understand and feel good about who you are. (Check out Chapter 16 for more tips on that.) You have plenty to be proud of! Remember that having LD, wearing glasses, having brown hair or freckles are all part of being human. When you like yourself, other people will be comfortable with you. Making and keeping friends takes work. But when you gain a friend, you will have a very special person in your life!

Continuing on the Trail

Congratulations! You've finished *Many Ways to Learn*. Now what? Well, we hope that you have a better understanding of what LD is and what you can do about yours. We hope you've learned a lot about yourself, too. Remember, this book is just the beginning of your climb. There's a lot more you can do and learn! At the back of the book, there is a list of resources for you and your parents to help learn more about LD.

As you move from grade to grade, you'll meet new challenges and achieve new successes. Remember what inspires every mountain climber: Each move you make brings you closer to your goal. As you strive for that goal, you have lots of help along the way. All you have to do is ask for it! When problems get in your way, use your tools to help. When you feel lost or tired, call upon your climbing team for support. Remember, the tools in this book and elsewhere won't help you unless you use them.

You live in a time when schools and colleges offer special programs to help kids with LD. LD need not stop you from succeeding. You have intelligence, you have strengths, and you have people around you who care.

You have everything you need to reach your mountain top. Good luck on your climb!

Climbing Resources

Books for Kids

DOING BETTER IN SCHOOL

Annie's Plan: Taking Charge of Schoolwork and Homework by Jeanne Kraus (Magination Press)

Get Organized Without Losing It by Janet Fox and Pamela Espeland (Free Spirit Publishing)

How to Be School Smart: Super Study Skills by Elizabeth James and Carol Barkin (Beech Tree Books)

How to Do Homework Without Throwing Up by Trevor Romain (Free Spirit Publishers)

The School Survival Guide for Kids With LD* (Learning Differences) by Rhonda Cummings and Gary Fisher (Free Spirit Publishing)

See You Later, Procrastinator! (Get It Done) by Pamela Espeland and Elizabeth Verdick (Free Spirit Publishing)

True or False? Tests Stink! by Trevor Romain and Elizabeth Verdick (Free Spirit Publishing)

DYSLEXIA AND OTHER KINDS OF LD

The Alphabet War: A Story About Dyslexia by Diane Burton Robb (Albert Whitman)

It's Called Dyslexia by Jennifer Moore-Mallinos (Barron's Educational Series)

Josh: A Boy With Dyslexia by Caroline Janover (iUniverse)

My Name Is Brain, Brian by Jeanne Betancourt (Scholastic)

That's Like Me: Stories About Amazing People With Learning Differences by Jill Lauren (Star Bright Books)

The Survival Guide for Kids With LD by Rhonda Cummings and Gary Fisher (Free Spirit Publishing)

ABOUT ADHD

Attention, Girls! A Guide to Learn All About Your AD/HD by Patricia O. Quinn, MD (Magination Press)

Putting on the Brakes: Understanding and Taking Control of Your ADD or ADHD, Second Edition by Patricia O. Quinn, MD, and Judith M. Stern, MA (Magination Press)

Putting on the Brakes Activity Book for Kids With ADD or ADHD, Second Edition by Patricia O. Quinn, MD, and Judith M. Stern, MA (Magination Press)

Learning to Slow Down and Pay Attention: A Book for Kids About ADHD, Third Edition by Kathleen Nadeau, PhD, and Ellen Dixon (Magination Press)

The Survival Guide for Kids With ADD and ADHD by John Taylor (Free Spirit Publishing)

FEELINGS AND BEHAVIOR

Being Me: A Kid's Guide to Boosting Confidence and Self-Esteem by Wendy L. Moss, PhD (Magination Press)

The Feelings Book: The Care & Keeping of Your Emotions by Lynda Madison, PhD (American Girl)

Mind Over Basketball: Coach Yourself to Handle Stress by Jane Weierbach, PhD, and Elizabeth Phillips-Hershey, PhD (Magination Press)

What-to-Do Guides for Kids™ by Dawn Huebner, PhD (Magination Press)

What to Do When You Worry Too Much: A Kid's Guide to Overcoming Anxiety

What to Do When You Grumble Too Much: A Kid's Guide to Overcoming Negativity

MAKING AND KEEPING FRIENDS

Cliques, Phonies, & Other Baloney by Trevor Romain (Free Spirit Publishing)

Making Choices and Making Friends by Pamela Espeland (Free Spirit Publishing)

We Can Get Along: A Child's Book of Choices by Lauren Murphy Payne, MSW, and Claudia Rohling, MSW (Free Spirit Publishing)

ABOUT YOUR BRAIN

The Great Brain Book: An Inside Look at the Inside of Your Head by H. P. Newquist, Keith Kasnot, and Eric Brace (Scholastic)

It's All in Your Head: A Guide to Your Brilliant Brain, Second Edition by Sylvia Funston and Jay Ingram (Maple Tree Press)

Books for Parents

The ADD/ADHD Checklist: A Practical Reference for Parents and Teachers, Second Edition by Sandra F. Rief, MA (Jossey Bass)

Basic Facts About Dyslexia and Other Reading Problems by Louisa Moats and Karen E. Dakin (International Dyslexia Association)

The Dyslexia Checklist: A Practical Reference for Parents and Teachers by Sandra F. Rief, MA, and Judith M. Stern, MA (Jossey Bass)

It's So Much Work to Be Your Friend: Helping the Child With Learning Disabilities Find Social Success by Richard Lavoie (Touchstone)

Late, Lost, and Unprepared: A Parent's Guide to Helping Children With Executive Functioning by Joyce Cooper-Kahn, PhD, and Laurie Dietzel, PhD (Woodbine)

The Misunderstood Child: Understanding and Coping With Your Child's Learning Disabilities, Fourth Edition by Larry B. Silver, MD (Three Rivers Press)

The Parent's Guide to Learning Disabilities by Stephen McCarney and Angela Bauer (Hawthorne Educational Services)

Thinking Organized for Parents and Children: Helping Kids Get Organized for Home, School and Play by Rhona Gordon (Thinking Organized)

Software

There are countless products on the market. We've listed a few here— you may want to do your own research as well.

FOR HELP WITH LOTS OF SUBJECTS

www.rocknlearn.com

Help students learn math, phonics, reading, social studies, test-taking strategies, writing, and science.

HELP WITH READING

www.reader-rabbit.com
Reading Blaster
www.knowledgeadventure.com/school

HELP WITH MATH

Activities and Games for Math Practice
www.softtouch.com/mathematics.aspx
Math Blaster
www.knowledgeadventure.com/mathblaster
MathPad
electronic numbers processor
www.synapseadaptive.com/intellitools/mathpad.html

WORD PREDICTION SOFTWARE

Co:Writer
www.donjohnston.com
SpeakQ
www.wordq.com

VOICE RECOGNITION

Dragon NaturallySpeaking
www.nuance.com

ORGANIZERS FOR WRITING

Draft:Builder
www.donjohnston.com
Kidspiration
www.inspiration.com

TEXT-TO-SPEECH SOFTWARE (WORD RECOGNITION)

Blio
www.blioreader.com
ClaroRead PLUS
www.clarosoftware.com
Kurzweil 3000
www.kurzweiledu.com
Read & Write Gold
www.readwritegold.com
ReadPlease
www.readplease.com

Write:OutLoud and Read:OutLoud
www.donjohnston.com.

KEYBOARDING PRACTICE

Mario Teaches Typing2
www.mobygames.com
Mavis Beacon Teaches Typing
www.broderbund.com
Sense-lang
www.sense-lang.org/
Type to Learn
www.sunburst.com

Gadgets

There are many products on the market. We've
listed a few here, but you may want to do your
own research as well.

ELECTRONIC DICTIONARIES

Franklin Talking Spell Checker
www.franklin.com
Wizcom Quicktionary Reading Pen
www.wizcomtech.com

SMARTPENS

Pulse Smartpen
Records audio as it records written text.
www.livescribe.com/smartpen

E-READERS

Intel Reader
kReader Mobile

TALKING CALCULATORS

Calc-U-Vue® Talking Calculator by Learning
Resources
Talking Calculator by Attainment Company

VARIABLE SPEED TAPE RECORDERS

Deskmate (with Variable Speed) by Panasonic
Handi Cassette II Stereo Recorder/Player by
SightConnection

WORD PROCESSORS

Fusion   www.writerlearning.com
NEO   www.neo-direct.com
Quick Pad
www.quickpad.com

Online Resources

READING LD

Downloadable Audio Books
www.loudlit.org
Phonics and Word Games
www.adrianbruce.com/reading/games.htm
Reading is Fundamental
www.rif.org/kids
Recording for the Blind and Dyslexic
www.rfbd.org
20 Roszel Road, Princeton, NJ 08540

ORGANIZATIONAL MATERIALS

Materials for students including structured
assignment notebooks and calendars.
www.successbydesign.com

ORGANIZATIONS

International Dyslexia Association (IDA)
www.interdys.org
40 York Road, 4th Floor, Baltimore, MD 21204
LD OnLine
www.LDOnline
Learning Disabilities Association of America
(LDA)
www.ldaamerica.org
4156 Library Road, Pittsburgh, PA 15234-1349
National Association for the Education of
African American Children with Learning
Disabilities (NAEAACLD)
www.aacld.org
P.O. Box 09521, Columbus, OH 43209
National Center for Learning Disabilities
(NCLD)
www.ld.org
381 Park Avenue South, Suite 1401, New
York, NY 10016
National Library Service for the Blind and
Physically Handicapped
www.loc.gov/nls
Smart Kids with Learning Disabilities, Inc.
www.smartkidswithld.org
38 Kings Highway North, Westport, CT 06880

Acknowledgments

The authors would like to thank Judy Hagemann for her always helpful advice and suggestions on technology and LD, and Naomi Baum-Skorija, MS, CCC-SLP, who generously contributed information on language-learning disabilities.

About the Authors

Judith Stern, MA, is an experienced teacher and educational consultant in private practice in Rockville, Maryland. She specializes in working with children who have learning disabilities and attention-deficit disorder as well as with their parents and teachers. She lectures nationally to professionals and parents on learning and attention problems, as well as improving children's study and organization skills. She is the co-author of four children's books on LD and ADHD and *The Dyslexia Checklist: A Practical Reference for Parents and Teachers*.

Uzi Ben-Ami, PhD, is a psychologist in private practice in Rockville, Maryland. He has worked extensively with children, parents, and schools as a certified school psychologist, and child and family therapist. Dr. Ben-Ami has evaluated and treated children and adolescents with learning disabilities throughout his career.

About the Illustrator

Hailing from the beautiful country of Wales, Carl Pearce claims to have spent the majority of his childhood outdoors and neck-deep in trouble. A rascal as a boy, he now enjoys spending time at the beach, drawing, doing photography, reading in the bath, and watching crazy movies. He doubts that he'll ever grow up!

About Magination Press

Magination Press publishes self-help books for kids and the adults in their lives. Magination Press is an imprint of the American Psychological Association, the largest scientific and professional organization representing psychologists in the United States and the largest association of psychologists worldwide.